# BREAKING BARRIERS TO DESIRE

**Polyamory, Polyfidelity and Non-monogamy — new approaches to multiple relationships**

*Edited by Kevin Lano and Claire Parry*

FIVE LEAVES PUBLICATIONS

# BREAKING THE BARRIERS TO DESIRE
## Polyamory, Polyfidelity and Non-monogamy – new approaches to multiple relationships

Published in 1995 by Five Leaves Publications, PO Box 81, Nottingham, NG5 4ER

©Kevin Lano and Claire Parry

ISBN 0 907123 36 8

# Contents

## Part I: **Polyamory in Practice**

| | |
|---|---:|
| **A Couple-Three: A Personal Essay** — Bernadette Lynn Bosky | 1 |
| **When Three is Not an Odd Number** — Claire Parry | 9 |
| **How to be not Monogamous** — Alison Rowan | 13 |
| **Life Story** — Jeff | 20 |
| **Mardi Gras** — Maria Pallotta-Chiarolli | 26 |
| **Group Sex** — Alison Rowan | 33 |
| **Life Story** — Rebecca | 36 |

## Part II: **Theory and Politics**

| | |
|---|---:|
| **Choosing Not to Choose: Beyond Monogamy, Beyond Duality** — Maria Pallotta-Chiarolli | 41 |
| **The History of Non-monogamous Lifestyles: A Historical and Cross-cultural Survey** — Kevin Lano | 68 |
| **Liberty in Chains: The Diaries of Anne Lister (1817–24)** — Emma Donoghue | 79 |
| **Clearly God Intended Polemics to be Threadbare: Some Christian Theological Justifications for Monogamy and Polygyny** — Jennifer Rycenga | 87 |
| **Friends Can't be Lovers: The Paradox of Monogamy** — Kevin Lano | 107 |

| | |
|---|---:|
| **References** | 113 |
| **Contributors** | 125 |
| **Glossary** | 127 |
| **Resources and Groups** | 129 |

# Preface

Polyamory and non-monogamy, whilst increasingly acknowledged aspects of relationships, have not yet been accepted as valid alternative ways of living. This book will aim to show that 'responsible non-monogamy' can be both a positive choice at a personal level, and a radicalising current in society, providing a true alternative to the dependence and exclusion of traditional monogamy, and the lack of responsibility and honesty in covert non-monogamy.

Responsible non-monogamy means a non-monogamous lifestyle or arrangement in which all the partners concerned are aware of and consent to the form of relationship – thus it is distinguished both from traditional monogamy and polygamy, and from the practice of serial monogamy together with secret affairs which is the mainstream of present Western society. The term *polyamory*: 'more loves than one' has become a generic term intended to cover all forms of responsible non-monogamy, and helps to emphasise that there is more than just sex at issue in non-monogamy.

The first part of the book is about 'doing it' – the practical experiences of people who have attempted to live in a polyamorous way. The second concerns 'theorising about it' – how non-monogamy relates to theories of sexuality, gender, religion and spirituality.

The history of non-monogamy has been hidden in much the same way that the history of homosexuality or of the working class has been concealed, since the history books have been written by and for upper class, heterosexual (in the West, usually Christian) men. Thus the book will attempt to uncover some of this history and describe historical antecedents for the current rise of interest in the polyamorous option, whilst recognising that previous versions of non-monogamy were often quite different in their aims and social context.

Bisexuality has often been regarded with scepticism and prejudice precisely because it appears to lead to non-monogamy: and this has been a greater challenge to many people than a different sexual orientation. Thus the recognition of the validity of responsible non-monogamy is actually a key element in the acceptance of bisexuality, and a number of articles in the book cover this subject. This is not to imply that every polyamorous person is inevitably bisexual, or even agrees with conventional sexuality labels, and the book also contains accounts from heterosexually and lesbian-identified people.

A wide variety of models for organising non-monogamous relationships exist and have been successfully applied. These include triads, polyfidelity (non-monogamous groups closed to sexual relationships outside the group), 'line marriages', open marriages and distributed commitment. Personal experiences of triads, open relationships and distributed commitment, and of other forms, are given in the first part of the book. It is a point of contention in the poly community as to whether 'swinging' can be regarded as responsible non-monogamy – we think that it can be, provided that the choices made are negotiated and consenting. The article on group sex explores this area in more detail.

The second part of the book provides a historical and political context for non-monogamous choices, and describes some well-known and not so well-known precursors to todays poly community. Finally, we provide an extensive bibliography, a glossary of terms, and details of existing support groups.

## Acknowledgement

The editors acknowledge the help of Francoise Gollain in preparing this book, and Nik Jardine and Trish Merrifield for the illustrations.

# Chapter 1

# A Couple-Three: A Personal Essay

**Bernadette Lynn Bosky**

In grade-school, long before I learned – and instantly adopted – the mid-south colloquialism "a couple-three," I liked that inexact and useful concept. In fact, I routinely used "couple" to mean anything more than one and less than "a few." "Well," my mother once said after I had asked for "a couple of" something and picked three, "If that's your idea of a couple, I'd hate to see you on your honeymoon!"

Neither of us dreamt how prophetic that would be. I now live in a committed triad with two men. I have lived with Arthur for thirteen years, and my romantic involvement with Kevin began over seven years ago. The three of us became a social unit within a year; and two-and-a-half years ago we moved in together as a full-time household. Neither Arthur nor Kevin is bisexual. They are not married to each other, as each is married to me, but they are family to each other. We share expenses, pool our resources, support and share in good times and bad. While keeping our individual differences and interests, we make plans as a household, spending our non-work time together far more often than not. Our relationship is still sexually open, but we rarely if ever take advantage of the opportunity.

At first glance, we don't seem to be the kind of people who would live a sexually-adventurous lifestyle. In fact, I've sometimes said that one advantage of living in a triad is that we can automatically be exotic and avant-garde, without having to *do* anything. Certainly, we tend to value consistency and security over the challenge of complicated interrelationships, a calm household over emotional gymnastics. We live in the suburbs of New York City, in an Italian-Catholic area, and we seem to be fully accepted in the casual, distantly friendly manner of neighbours today. In many ways, we are like a rather ordinary couple, for large values of two.

In other ways, of course, that isn't the case and can never be. As my spouse Kevin has put it, "As long as there are three of us, we will always be odd." As with other forms of societal values and prejudices, the orientation of our culture towards the couple is so pervasive that it can be hard to notice – until you are (or sufficiently listen to) someone who is on the other side.

We have been fortunate in many areas of life, and as a result we have had it much easier than other triads might. Since we can afford our own house, we don't have to worry about our landlord kicking out the "third person not related by blood," as happened to friends of ours. Living first in an enlightened college town and then in a multicultural metropolitan area, we haven't experienced the prejudice described by friends of ours in smaller towns or more conservative states. Nor do we have to worry about the reaction of our employers, a very real fear for many multiple marriages: Arthur and I freelance from home, while Kevin's office – where he got a job largely through friends in the science-fiction community – is truly liberal and welcomes both me and Arthur at the company Christmas party.

Still, even when there is no overt judgement, there is the iron law of the default, the constant *de facto* privileging that comes in a world built for couples. I'm sure this is not actually directed at triads (or any multiple-adult household), any more than it is directed at single people; but in each case, the effect is to make our lives that much harder, to make us seem that much more like outsiders. Carnival rides are built for two, and Valentine's dinner specials are two-for-one; commercial forms have room for two names, legal forms for one next-of-kin (unless it's your parents). It's not that these things can't be circumvented – they can, and we are usually successful in doing so – but that no matter how well it is dealt with, the message of exclusion is there.

The strongest example of this in our personal life may be marriage itself. With enough ingenuity (and, again, money), three people can have all of the component benefits of marriage, and we have done many and plan to do the rest: sign powers of attorney and appropriately-drafted wills, legally own property together, even have a public social event sanctifying and commemorating our union. Yet

# A Couple-Three

not only is this much more expensive and complicated than legal marriage, it will never actually *be* the same thing. Because, the not-so-covert message goes, you can "really" marry only one person at a time.

More than having to accommodate to a world that does not fit our number, or even being denied legal opportunities and protections that other families have, I think relationships like ours suffer from our invisibility. Such households are uncommon, and there are many ways in which a marriage of more than two people can go wrong. But it can work well, too, in many more ways and much more often than most people imagine. People organise themselves in units of "a couple-three" – more than two, but less than a group – all the time, even if the romantic mythology, of the couple or of "buddy" pairings, tends to obscure this.

In fact, during the time in my life when I used "a couple" to mean "three," there was a more serious predictor of my current life: through most of grade school and all of junior high, my sister and I had the same "best friend." We did everything together, from studying to playing superhero as The Tremendous Trio; and while we had squabbles, as any schoolchildren will, there was never any consistent tendency for two to gang up on – let alone shut out – a third. On the contrary, my sister and I and our friend Nancy seemed to disagree less, and settle our agreements more amicably, than my sister and I did alone.

It was only years later, after college, that I even realized this was considered remarkable. An informal survey of my friends certainly did make it seem uncommon. Now I have come full circle, and I wonder how unusual such social and emotional constellations are, and how much they are instead simply ignored, re-defined as two plus one, or two plus two, instead of acknowledged as a stable, ongoing three or more.

As I have looked around me, I have continued to notice more and more examples of these groupings. They are rarely permanent, but they are often very long-lasting – and on average, the ties among a small cluster of college friends, closeness of two couples, or bonds between a couple and their mutual friend may last longer than the average marriage. Most of the relationships do not include sex (except within couple sub-sets), but my guess is that the sex would be much, much more common if the culture were more conducive to it. And it is probably already more common, in a sad and dishonest way, than is openly acknowledged.

This makes it all the more amazing that households of more than two adults, as a recognised alternative lifestyle, are still almost invisible culturally, but that is definitely the case. In sharp contrast to gays, there is less hostility towards people in multiple marriages, but there is even less acknowledgement and support.

Please don't get me wrong, here: social attention can be very dangerous, too, and there is no doubt in my mind that being ignored and feeling totally isolated is much better than, say, being beaten to death. Still, there have been times when I would have given quite a bit – though definitely not *that* much – to be able to turn to the kind of literature, support community, role models, and advice on dealing with the world at large that gays can now find. Instead, I have discovered that if we want that kind of identity and support, we will have to *build* it, for ourselves and for others.

In the only book on triads and threesome sex, *Threesomes*, Arno Karlen comments, "I began to wonder if anything on threesomes wasn't moralising, proselytising, or guesswork." With a few exceptions, this could be applied, in my jaundiced view, to all treatments of marriage among more than two people. The subject is understandably a strong one emotionally, and most authors have either pathologised or idealised the whole experience, with their work suffering accordingly. Karlen's book is an exception to this, as is Marcia Seligson's *Options*, but both of them show another problem: the number of sexual and domestic arrangements possible for more than two people is so vast, and the number of books written on the topic is so small, that there is a tendency to look at too wide a field and sacrifice more specific or characteristic analysis.

Moreover, much of the writing about triad and group marriages barely manages to avoid the most common mistake that the general public makes on the topic: overemphasising the sex. Yes, if it had not been for sexual attraction, our *menage* would never have come about; and certainly sex helps smooth and assure our connections, as it does in any marriage of fewer people. Yet as any married person will tell you, the ups and downs have a lot less to do with the sex and a lot more to do with the life which it reflects and fits into: the tears and laughter, the bills and good news, keeping the home working and accommodating each other's foibles.

In my more self-deprecating moods, I sometimes say that our triad works so well because it takes three of us to make one adult couple. At other times, I see the same link, but think of it as a comment on the nigh-impossible demands of marriage in a nuclear family, rather than on any inadequacies we might have. Arthur and I were never a self-enclosed pair, and we have always turned to family and friends for emotional support and help, as well as for enjoyment and recreation. Still, having a core household of three people provides us with that much more strength to draw on all the time, that much more flexibility and give in our life together. Not only does this make for more security and joy within our household, it means we have more to share with those outside the household as well, from shoulders to cry on through strong backs for moving furniture.

During times of tension between two members of a triad, the presence of a third person can create even more involved messes, but it can also – instead – provide an oasis of calm during stormy arguments. This can include both reliable general reassurance (to both people arguing) and the benefits of a knowledgeable but more objective perspective on things. My spouse Arthur has often said that he never understood how two people could determine which of their views was more realistic. With us, the third opinion might not always be more correct in itself, but the perspective it gives is always useful, leading to a more accurate understanding overall. We also find that the mere presence of someone who loves both people helps keep conflicts civil: for one thing, the innocent third party doesn't deserve shouting within the home!

When more than two adults are involved, all of the processes of home and family life are basically the same, yet the details can be very different. That is, the same jobs must be done, and one experiences the same kinds of emotions and challenges, leading to the same kinds of joys and sorrows; and always, some will do better at this and some will manage it more poorly. Yet the same could be said about handling any computer, from a Kaypro to a Cray, while details differ so much that even knowing one word-processing program will not necessarily prepare you to use another. In my experience, what I learned about being a good spouse in a couple has never hindered me being a good spouse in a triad, but it often has been inadequate. We had to make new models, come up with creative solutions – and we had to do it almost entirely on our own.

A community and support structure is just now beginning to spread. It often uses the term "polyamory," a pleasant and useful neologism that covers a wide range of people with "many loves," definitely including marriages of more than two. On the Internet, for instance, I can communicate with people interested in polyamorous life, some of whom are in multiple marriages older than ours. The feeling of belonging is wonderful, and deep friendships can be formed (I was recently an attendant in the wedding of an Internet friend to her second husband), but I am even more delighted by the opportunity to share the nuts and bolts, the practical and emotional details of our lives.

We discovered this community, however, after we had mostly grappled with the basic issues of our own. Arthur and I had known a few triads through science fiction fandom; otherwise, I'm not sure I would even have seen it as a possibility when the situation did present itself. However, the examples were so few, and the differences between them and us so major, that I still felt very much alone. We had sympathetic friends who were more than willing to listen, but that cannot compare with being able to talk with others who are charting the same territory.

As the three of us decided to make commitments and form something beyond a couple (and their single friend), I spent about three years almost constantly conscious of and working on our relationship(s): assessing and talking, excited and scared – in some ways an invigorating thing, but incredibly demanding. I honestly do not know if I could have done it if I had been employed full-time, or if our natures had been only slightly different. I was in therapy for other reasons, and my counsellor definitely helped, though we joked about his nervousness at the newness of it all too. Slowly, the feeling of being on a high-wire diminished. Of course we still work to make our love go well, but things feel basically settled now, for which I literally thank God. I never doubt that all the work was worth it, but I would not want to have to keep it up, either.

In my experience, it is not so much that following couple-based patterns will get you into trouble with more than one partner, as much as that you can be repeatedly caught up short by situations in which it is simply impossible. Many of our friends have commented that this produces a wonderful freedom from the burden of old social roles, and that is true. Yet *having* to be free and creative, and being unable to rely on habit and convention if you want to, can be its own kind of burden. The best of both worlds would be a blend of freedom and security, including being able to look at a number of possible role models and incorporate a number of different, at-least-somewhat-tested elements in one's own relationship(s). I hope this will happen for others because of work being done now, including projects like this book.

One thing that needs to be done is the further development of the terminology. What exists is all helpful, but there is far too little of it. For instance, even within the polyamory community we have not come across a general name for Kevin and Arthur's relation to each other, though we have come to use my therapist's term "co-husband."

# A Couple-Three

"Triangular" vs. "linear" is a useful way to indicate whether (respectively) all people in a triad share sex, or two people share sex with the third but not each other – but there are no equivalent terms for levels or kinds of sexual involvement (A shares sex with B while C is also sharing, but not alone; B sexually enjoys cuddling A but does more extensive sexual stuff only with C), let alone for lines of emotional, social, financial, or other connection.

Probably, some terms can be culled from the anthropology of polygamous cultures, while others could be neologisms (like "polyamory") or new uses for general words (like "linear"). Already this is happening, along with borrowing from the terminology of gay and other alternative communities (especially "coming out," a useful term for a concept we find vital also). Perhaps the biggest hindrance to this work now is the tendency to argue, as soon as the terms are defined, over which approach is better, or at least to covertly assign superior value to one or another term. This may be inevitable, but the more it is avoided, the more quickly we can reach a useful *descriptive* vocabulary.

Similarly, we need to record and share as various as possible a range of approaches and role models for polyamorous living, encouraging people to find what is right for them. The emphasis must be on finding the right match to one's own situation and temperament, rather than what is "better." In addition, we need to both create and discover or identify even more kinds of basic approaches to households with more than two adults. As far as I can tell, the three major inspirational templates now seem to be the pastoral commune, the novels of Robert A. Heinlein, and the self-sufficient nuclear family – none of them well suited to be the whole basis of something practical and successful, though all can contribute useful and even invaluable elements.

In practice, the flexibility and inventiveness shown by people forming polyamorous households can be quite delightful. Most of those we know have idiosyncratic terms they have adopted – developed out of the relationships and personalities involved – which have both specific meanings and deep emotional associations. This is not easily applicable in the more general sense I have spoken of, but by examining the more personal terms and roles we can learn what issues, distinctions, and concepts we might look for in a more categorical analysis.

Our own major invention was to think of Mom, Dad, and Junior as identifications that floated among the three of us, a technique that helped us both to acknowledge and to create a balance among us in terms of the traditional family roles. Thus, Kevin might be Dad as he arrived from work and picked us up to go out to eat, Arthur would be Dad as he figured out the bill and laid down the cash, and I would be Dad as I drove home. (When I explained this to one feminist friend, twice she said, "And you're always Mom, right?" and twice I had to correct her: "Oh God no! How awful!") Our one rule is "no single parents": it takes two people to be responsible enough for one to be mostly taken care of, and trying to do that with only one other around is an imposition. Obviously, this would not work for everyone — if nothing else, it would need some adjustment, or at least clarification, for a triad that also has real children to raise. The most important thing is what it did for us, leading us to look at how traditional family roles did and did not apply to us, what aspects of them we wanted to use and what we wanted to reject.

Finally, as a community grows, it will inevitably fulfil the basic purpose of sharing experiences. While my temperament and profession lead me to care about terminology and psycho-social roles, I have to say that this level of personal exchange is probably the most important kind of discussion there can be. How do you set up living-quarters: one home or more? shared or separate bedrooms? If there are children, are all participants equal parents? is it important who the genetic parents are? is it even *known* who the genetic parents are? How are finances handled? Housework? How do decisions remain open to all without the process becoming unwieldy? In each case, the answers will differ, but they will all be equally vital, both to the people involved and — as sparks to their own ideas, if nothing else — to those forming new households in the future.

As I have said, our own triad is now pretty settled and secure — it is, at any rate, no more frightening, awesome, exhilarating, and profoundly challenging than any other marriage. In some ways, I feel that to truly share your life with another human being is so incredible a thing that nothing can make it *much* more so, even upping the number of people. Still, a triad — or any kind of multiple marriage — has some of its own unique answers to that universal challenge, and these need to be discussed in the open, in ways that have hardly yet begun.

Even this essay is not so much a first attempt as it is a call to action, but I hope that I have at least indicated both what we should be studying and why. The first step in understanding something, after all, is to really *look* at it — or even, if the prevailing opinion is otherwise, to apprehend that it exists at all and is worthy of our attention.

# Chapter 2

# When Three is Not an Odd Number

**Claire Parry**

It is perhaps no surprise that many bisexuals react negatively to the concept of "threesomes" – it smacks of the seventies image of bisexuality, of the shock-horror of "kinky" sex seen through monogamous heterosexual eyes, as well as the porn images of two passive women performing for a man's pleasure. The way in which we have been used as scapegoats is linked in many people's minds with promiscuity and irresponsibility. A sharp division is drawn between monogamy (= sensible, normal, mature) and promiscuity (= irresponsible, perverted, immature) which in turn creates a false picture of sexuality – everyone is either living in a state of cosy, domesticated fidelity or jumping into bed with the nearest person to hand at any available opportunity. We all *know* that these are stereotypes, but the existence of these stereotypes affects both our own self-image and the attitudes of others.

A "relationship" is invariably interpreted as being between two people: it is then labelled as either hetero- or homosexual. The couple is always taken as the norm for relationships, even though the concept of monogamy as a social institution has long been under attack from several quarters. Even some lesbians and gays who pride themselves on their radical politics and rejection of heterosexual norms have relationships which are almost marriage-like and regard monogamy as an ideal. Neither is the use of the terms "boyfriend" and "girlfriend" to denote exclusive social and sexual possession of another, confined to heterosexual couples.

Even if bisexuals do have concurrent relationships, it is usually assumed that there will be a strict division between the straight and lesbian/gay worlds – hence the popular image of the bisexual as an outwardly straight, respectable person who conducts his or her "unacceptable" affairs in deadly secret. The very word "bisexual" hints at a split personality, forced to lead a double life in view of the prejudices of straight society and the suspicion of the lesbian/gay subculture. But what of those whose lives do not fit into these patterns?

The "triangular" relationship is nearly always associated with a destructive, decadent lifestyle – the stuff of melodrama and tragedy. Behind this image lies once again the social propaganda for heterosexuality and monogamy, intensified by the media reaction to the AIDS crisis. The horror of any lifestyle which seems to threaten the fabric of conventional society is so great that it is instantly damned as irresponsible, sick and "unnatural". I am not trying to portray everyone who chooses a monogamous relationship as hopelessly reactionary – the fact is that our society prizes monogamy to such an extent that the notion of "choice" becomes little more than a liberal myth: it is not a real or informed choice.

In a society where women have long been regarded as men's "property", it is only to be expected that everything will be geared towards monogamy, from the legal system to the commercial exploitation of "romance" and dating agencies which promise to find your "perfect partner". As a dire warning to those who fail to conform to these standards, society has waged a constant war against the bad guys and girls: the "slag" who sleeps around and refuses to be dependent on any one man; the lesbian who rejects men completely; the man who refuses to play out the expected macho role. Lesbians and gays in particular are only accepted (if at all) by straight society if they live in monogamous partnerships – they can then be dismissed as "just like us really, except that they're queer". However, the state still refuses to recognize their relationships on an equal par with heterosexual ones – there is a hierarchy of monogamy graded by sexuality!

So what kind of propaganda do the proponents of compulsory monogamy use to shore up their arguments? It's interesting that two of the charges usually levelled against those who advocate non-monogamous relationships are the same as those typically aimed at bisexuals – the accusations of "irresponsibility" and "immaturity". One phrase often used is "you're only experimenting". *Only* experimenting? Isn't experimentation the way in which we learn, grow and

# When Three is Not an Odd Number

develop as a species? Perhaps for some people it's safer to stagnate. As for responsibility regarding safer sex, I feel that non-monogamy brings a greater responsibility in negotiating safer sexual practices (and, where necessary, contraception) – it's all too easy to become complacent in a relationship which is viewed as monogamous. The charge of immaturity is likewise one which should perhaps be laid elsewhere – with those who swallow wholesale the myths of Mills and Boon dreams of lifelong fidelity and marital bliss.

Another commonly voiced objection to non-monogamy (and one which I have heard from people of all sexualities) is that it is very nice in theory but takes a lot of effort in practice. To a certain extent I would agree with this: the effort of maintaining a balance between your relationships so that no party feels unfairly treated or left out can be considerable. The question of living arrangements is also of importance here: if the situation is a true "menage a trois", i.e. with all three partners living together, the practical considerations will be different from a set-up where all three live alone but within easy travelling distance of each other, and different again from a relationship in which two members live together and the third lives in a communal house in a different town – to give just a few examples of situations which I have encountered. There is no hard-and-fast rule as there are no rules set by society for such relationships. We have to make the rules ourselves, and it is always more difficult to construct our own relationship structures than it is to follow a pre-existing pattern. In addition, I would argue that monogamy also requires a lot of effort: it is simply because monogamous relationships are encouraged by society that we tend to see them as "natural" and therefore easier.

Even within the realm of the purely sexual, there are very few positive images of three-way relationships: the image that immediately springs to mind is that of the porn magazines, with the "lesbian" couple inviting a straight man into their bed to "fulfil" them both and to perform for his titillation. Thus the man, whatever his sexuality, involved in a triad with two women, is faced with several sets of stereotypes. To straight men he is either the "super stud" who has two women at once or something of a weirdo because he sleeps with women who have sex with each other. To some lesbians he would be viewed as an exploiter and invader of lesbian space. Similarly, the woman involved in a triad with two men may be seen as either a "slut" or a silly, pathetic woman who is being exploited for male pleasure. To counter these stereotypes I can only respond with my own experiences: the joy of seeing two people I love make love to each other; each one of us taking turns to be the centre of attention and joking about whose turn it was to be the filling in the sandwich; feeling like a group instead of a couple; above all, knowing that what we were doing was not shallow and immature, but creative, meaningful and constructive.

I feel that despite the apparent difficulties in constructing non-monogamous relationships, it is ultimately worth the effort. In my experience, too many people give up after one negative experience (which, on closer questioning, usually turns out to be a case of cheating within an apparently monogamous relationship rather than an openly non-monogamous one). I have had bad experiences of non-monogamous relationships, but I can honestly say that the good has outweighed the bad. For me, non-monogamy is where the personal and the political connect in a very powerful way. Although I do not believe we can change society simply by an individual "choice" of relationship, I do feel that the social institution of compulsory monogamy must be broken down in order for genuine social transformation to take place. Here I part company with those who place their hopes for a fairer society in the legalization of lesbian and gay marriage, as I feel this still privileges monogamy and leaves non-monogamous, or indeed celibate, people of all sexualities as second-class citizens. Perhaps most importantly, non-monogamy is the way in which as a bisexual I can truly live my sexuality and construct a better way of relating to those I love as friends, allies and partners.

# Chapter 3

# How To Be Not Monogamous

**Alison Rowan**

I am non-monogamous and have been for most of my sexually active life. For a while I thought I might be polyamorous, or some other word that made my lifestyle sound better, more positive, but I decided that it didn't fit. I call myself non-monogamous because the only constant and distinguishing fact about this part of my life is that I am not monogamous, I don't do things that way, the way that is expected; and after all if that weren't the expected way there would be nothing remarkable about me and this book would not exist. For reasons I still don't understand monogamy is not only the norm, but in spite of many changes in the way we think about sexuality is still almost totally unchallenged, and that's why what follows is a blatant piece of propaganda.

There are many, many ways to run your sex life and only one of them is monogamy, which is why I am surprised when people ask me why I'm not monogamous (well not surprised – I've had too much of it for that, but still taken aback). Surely the question should be about why they are? I have found, on the whole, that people don't actually want to know about non-monogamy. They are remarkably uninterested when I try to explain the differences between a committed open relationship and just living in the same flat as one of your lovers (a distinction they cannot comprehend) or between that and being single but occasionally, or often, having sex with friends or strangers (which many people can't see as non-monogamy at all, even though it's clearly not monogamy, either). What most people seem to want is not this kind of discussion. What they actually want to know is why I'm not like them.

Of course this question isn't the worst one by any means, just possibly the hardest to answer because it takes me directly up against a whole slew of assumptions. I can take it as an honest enquiry from most people – many of whom genuinely don't have any idea where to start the discussion, and I will do my best to tell them about my beliefs and why I live the way I do. But what really gets to me is the endless succession of questions that inevitably seem to follow, and which show exactly how hard it's going to be to explain – the ones about don't I think that I might want to commit myself to somebody some day (yes, thank you, I already have) about isn't sex without affection a bit depressing? (yes, I had some of that, a long time ago when I was trying to be monogamous for a while, and yes, it was horrible). Don't you get jealous? (yes, sometimes, but I also get jealous of my partner's job, and I don't require that they give that up); the question about ... well it all sounds quite "fun" (and what a lot of disapproval they can pack into a word like fun), but can you give me any examples of non-monogamous relationships that actually *work*?

This last is the point at which my questioners usually get stuck, and it took me a long time to work out why. At first I would try to answer it on their own terms by describing mine and some of my friends' relationships, and assuring my questioner that we were living a model life. I was lucky enough to meet a couple who had been together in an open marriage for twenty years and some men who had been living together in a gay threesome for eleven and I quoted their lives and those of other "successes" I had known with enthusiasm in all these arguments.

And then I began to give up.

Two things dawned on me about this argument was going nowhere. One was that I was arguing my case using their criteria for success (of which more later), and the other was that there are simply more of them than there are of us, and while this state of affairs prevails they will be able to keep asking us for examples until we run out. My married couple were dismissed as "swingers", and in any case they were straight and did I have any gay examples. The gay threesome was dismissed as being "merely promiscuous" (and this by people who had never seemed homophobic to me before). Anyway they didn't want to know about my model examples, they wanted to know about me.

## How To Be Not Monogamous

It's sometimes hard to tell genuine curiosity from prurient interest.

Even in the cause of non-monogamy I was unable and unwilling to disguise some of the real facts of my life at that time. And so I had it pointed out to me that my relationships were far from perfect and that I had been known to complain about my partners (so had they, of course). Finally when a friend's open relationship broke up and she decided to try being monogamous I was asked if I was going to do the same thing "to save my relationship". She seemed to have no doubt about which relationship I should save, oddly enough. I decided then that I was not going to try to justify myself anymore.

What I am prepared to do, though, is try to explain. And the reason I want to do this is that there are some things I really want explained to me: some things that bother me every time I see a monogamous assumption in action no matter how much I should be used to them (and I'm talking about monogamous assumptions, not relationships – it's the assumptions that get you every time). Maybe if I try to describe some of these things I might be able to let other people get a glimpse of what non-monogamy is like – for me ...

What's it like being non-monogamous? One thing it's like is always being able to talk about people you fancy with people you are sleeping with. It disturbs me deeply when I see couples sniping at each other about this; even, or perhaps especially, when it's meant to be a joke. You know, the kind of "ha, ha, only serious" joke that upholds everyone's (presumed) values and leaves them feeling more secure. When I'm feeling skittish I enjoy sharing loud opinions about cute men with a boyfriend because it winds people up so much (on two counts). On bad days, though, I can be heard nagging my friends with, "What, do you really mind her fancying your mate? Don't you trust her? What if it were Brett Anderson? What if it were me?" This invariably achieves nothing.

Being non-monogamous means that an offer of sex from someone you care deeply about becomes a source of celebration instead of (as all forms of literature insist) an agonising decision about your current relationship and their current relationship and the beginning, in fact, of a hackneyed soap plot. Where would literature be without infidelity, anyway, or Eastenders? What if Grant had said, "No, of course I don't mind you sleeping with my brother while I'm in prison, or anyone else for that matter – after all, it's not as if I'm going to be any worse off – how about that Michelle? I've always thought she's cute." Yes, being non-monogamous can often be a lot like being invisible.

It's like that when I read questionnaires in Marie Claire and other such supposedly sexually advanced publications that ask me have I ever been "unfaithful". I found a survey recently that I diligently filled in because it gave me the option of being bisexual (a rare enough thing in itself) only to find that I had the choice of being "unfaithful" according to their definition on paper or of actually being unfaithful to my girlfriend in my definition by failing to mention her at all. In a way non-monogamy is more invisible than bisexuality in that I honestly don't think that any of these magazines even realise there are people like me for whom words like "unfaithful" and concepts like "having an affair" are meaningless.

One thing non-monogamy is not like, sadly, is having an endless succession of lovers. Obviously it helps your score, in the crudest sense, to not have to turn people down just because you've got one lover already (in fact I was once told that the reason I was "easy" was that I was so ugly that I had to take every shag going). But not being single (another word that needs redefining) can make you a distinctly unattractive proposition in some people's eyes. Many bisexual women can tell of lesbians whose first reaction to women with male partners is not one of sisterly acceptance and while some men's attitude to a woman with a girlfriend is more enthusiastic, it's not necessarily the sort of enthusiasm I want to have to deal with. Threesomes are fine and good; the assumption that a threesome is all you're looking for, or that your consent includes your partner's, isn't.

Other, more well-meaning, people ask me repeatedly whether my partner will mind. This has been known to go on right up to, and into, bed, so that sometimes I wish I had had the foresight to get a signed statement to that effect. I doubt it would have helped, though, since this is essentially a guilt-ridden litany and has to do with the fact that it is difficult for people to believe that they are taking part in a fair and consensual situation instead of one of the soap plots mentioned earlier (it's hard to blame them, when that's all most people have ever been allowed to see). This disbelief is evinced by some of the bizarre qualms they come up with. We shouldn't do it in "his" (read our) bed, under "his" (read my) roof, when he's in town (he might come back), when he's not in town (because his backs turned), if my potential lover works with him (she'd have to face him in the morning) or if my date gets a sudden, irrational fear that it might all go horribly wrong.

I don't want to give the impression that I never get any lovers, though. I have had quite a few. Not as many as some people would like me to have had to prove either my bisexuality or my non-monogamy, but many more than some people – especially, but by no means exclusively, my parents – consider right. I do know that I have slept with more people than I would have done had I been monogamous and that, incidentally, my non-monogamy has "saved" more than one of my live-in relationships from ending sooner than it did, and more importantly saved me from what might have been disastrous moves to join the lust object of the moment on the grounds (from the gospel according to monogamy) that whoever your libido pulls you most strongly towards must be The One For You. (I know some monogamous people would deny this, but I'd like to know what else they mean when they say you "just know".)

There have been long periods when I haven't had any other lovers, though. Either through none being available or through my own disinclination to do anything about it. These have been times when I have found it particularly hard to explain to others that I am still non-monogamous. To me non-monogamy is a potential; admittedly, like bisexuality, it is a potential that I enjoy acting on often, but it is certainly not something that will atrophy through disuse. Even at times when I feel less inclined towards sex it hasn't occurred to me that I either should be or somehow already am monogamous. This is partially because I know that I am bound to want other lovers eventually, or that my partner will (and I don't see any need to limit their options just because I don't fancy anyone else at the moment); but it is at least as much to do with the many other less obvious advantages that non-monogamy offers. Many of which are to do with the way we think about sex.

Non-monogamy is about taking sex down from the pedestal that most people keep it on and bringing it into the realm of reality. And as soon as you look at sex as a real activity instead of a mythical quality you begin to ask what makes it so different from activities like eating and conversation. Why should sex of all things be the thing that breaks up relationships and causes such jealousy when a good conversation can go deeper, TV can steal more of your attention, and chess (as I found towards the end of one relationship) can take your lover away from you for longer. The answers are less than obvious. Sex seems to be treated in such an odd way in this society that people are endlessly tying themselves in knots simply trying to describe their own beliefs about it. On the one hand it is considered sacred (else why cement your agreements about who to have it with in church?) and on the other it is so dirty that half of our "dirty words" refer to it. We are forever being hyped as a "naturally monogamous" species, and yet our monogamy is hedged about with regulations and suspicions of failure as if it were the most difficult thing in the world to achieve. Sex is supposed to be no fun without True Love and yet obviously people will do anything for more of this sad experience, as we treat our sexuality like a train that is about to run away with us; out of control and wrecking lives as it goes.

There is one more thing that non-monogamy, or my constant defence of it, has taught me, and that is about the success of relationships. This actually came to me after running a workshop on non-monogamy where out of 30 people, at least half said that they had tried non-monogamy once, "but it had failed". This phrase got stuck in my mind until I had to work out what was wrong with it. What did they mean by failed? What does anybody mean by the word when they're talking about relationships? They mean the relationship ended. Which is very odd when you come to think of it. A meal is a failure because it doesn't taste nice, not because you ran out of food to eat, but a relationship can "fail" even if it's fun all the way through, because a meal isn't supposed to last forever and a relationship is if you're monogamous. But if you're not monogamous this just doesn't work anymore. In order to make the model fit you first have to take one of your relationships and call it the central one (and this is only true of *one* sort of non-monogamy), this is the one that's supposed to last forever. But that would mean, unless you plan on living in quite literally an eternal triangle (or polygon of your choice) that all your other relationships and sexual encounters are failures because they can't last as long. Not only that, but that they are *planned* to be failures. Why would anyone do that? Either all non-monogamous people are deep down trying to punish themselves for past sins, a theory belied by the amount of fun some of us are having, or our definition of failure in relationships is broken.

I recommend that non-monogamous people abandon longevity as the sole measure of the success of a relationship, and instead turn back to quality (of which longevity may be a part, since more of a good thing is often good), which is good enough for meals, parties, and works of literature. That way we can allow more than one of the relationships in our lives to be a success and we stand in no danger of having our successes re-written as failures the moment they are over. We are also then a little safer from the monogamous world which demands success as a proof of the validity of our lives.

For myself, the joys I have found in non-monogamous relationships are often independent of duration. For short relationships and "one night stands" there is the simple pleasure both of the sex itself, and of the knowledge that sex *can* be part of how I relate to people without "spoiling a beautiful friendship". In longer relationships I find it reassuring that my partner is staying with me even though they can and do seek other people. I enjoy group sex and I enjoy talking to all my friends, including my partners, about their sex lives and who they fancy this week. And I enjoy most of all the feeling, after a Catholic upbringing that encouraged me to feel ashamed, that my sex life belongs to *me*, not to the law, not to the church and not even to my partners, except incidentally. My ethics, and my promises, are mine to make and to keep.

# Chapter 4

# Life Story

**Jeff**

I was born in 1925 in Minneapolis Minnesota. At the time my parents were still married, however my father divorced my mother when I was four years old. I am of English and Scotch Irish heritage. My mother's family came from St. Albans Vermont and my father"s family from the Hudson River valley in New York state. I grew up in the academic neighbourhood of the University of Minnesota. My father was working on his PhD in history at the time. My impressions of my early childhood were of my mother's hatred of men as a group and her manipulation of men as individuals. To keep afloat during the depression, we took in boarders and I have the distinct recollection of one of our woman boarders beating her son with a belt. This left a lasting impression on me until I was in the military and my views were changed. Early on I became a protector of children against others who might victimise tease and taunt them on the way home from school. I don't recall any early sexual experiences except a Sunday school teacher who groped me at a picnic. My recollection was that the experience was pleasant and I thought nothing of it until recently as the issue of child abuse has been raised. In choir camp the older adolescent boys had us 12 year olds engage in mock coitus. We thought little of it as we had younger boys do the same.

In high school I was not athletic but was a leader academically and in student activities. I was instructed in the art of masturbation by my neighbourhood friend and we engaged in mutual masturbation as we fantasized about the girls in our class. He was also the captain of the football team and to this day I am not certain whether I was

# Life Story

fantasizing about him as well.

I dated girls in my class and as most adolescent boys bragged about my conquests which were limited. My sexual activity was mostly heavy necking and petting which reflected the mores of the time (1943).

Upon graduation from high school in 1943, I went immediately into the Army and ended up in an Infantry Company consisting mostly of men from Southern United States except for the handful of us pre college men. In this unit there was a lot of horse play and talk of masturbation but no actual conscious homoerotic behaviour. My close friends were more interested in going to town and doing the burlesque shows that then were in vogue. For the men in the unit who were illiterate, I would write letters home at their dictation. These letters were pretty steamy and included both language and activity that challenged my imagination. All were heterosexual however. Although I bonded with these men and really was fond of them, I never felt the intimacy had sexual overtones. The only experience I had which in retrospect might be considered homoerotic occured in a foxhole. S was a violinist in civilian life, frail and sensitive. The night sounds on the perimeter got to him and he was shaking with wet cold and fear. I could feel him tremble against me. I took him in my arms and held him. We warmed and steadied one another. I think he placed his head upon my shoulder. He cried. The memory stays with me since I have had this nurturing experience again in my lifetime.

My closest friend was a squirrel hunter from Arkansas. We would wrestle and play like a couple of bear cubs on the ground. We admired one another for our uniqueness, and in retrospect probably loved one another. After I left the unit I never saw him again. I returned to the United States to prepare for the United States Military Academy, however I held only an alternate appointment. Upon returning to civilian life, I was 22 years old. Within a week I entered college, joined a fraternity, and entered wholeheartedly to college social life which I managed to squeeze into my academic and activity schedule. I was in a concentrated Law course, and also active in student affairs. I dated every weekend, enjoyed the company of women, and engaged in the usual petting of the period. I was not as aggressive as most males, and was fearful of unwanted pregnancies. In my junior year, I spent the summer in England (1948) on a study project and the whole group socialised together. I fell in love with one girl of our group but all the men did as well. During this time period I started a travel business to finance my return trip to Europe as I had fallen in love with travel. I graduated with attachments and no hint of bisexuality.

At the time I was married I was the typical American suburban husband. We had a free standing home in the near suburbs, three children, attended Indian Guides with the two boys, and Boy Scouts as well. In the travel industry, I did encounter a number of persons who I thought might be gay or homosexual as it was known at that time. My first cousin was a lesbian and the family did not make an issue of it. However she tended to move in different circles. During this period from age 28 to 40 my mind was primarily concerned with operating a business. I did travel a great deal, particularly to Europe, but was usually too exhausted for sexual exploration. Our friends were primarily married couples and our activities focussed around church. We are Episcopalian and the issues at that time were primarily racial and not sexual.

In 1967, I entered volunteer public service. This as well as my business kept me busy. At the age of 40, I went to Germany for Carnival with a travel industry friend. Needless to say the Fasching is a wild affair and we celebrated with reckless abandon ... including a wild night at the Berlin Hilton with two ladies of the night. We had picked them up at the Sports Palace; I remember the event since for all the revelry, the sex was disappointing. Actually I was having a better time drinking with my male friend. Later that year we were together in San Juan Puerto Rico and we happened on a mixed dance hall of gay and straight couples. We danced together, he and I thinking nothing of it at the time. Yet in retrospect I was moving toward bisexuality almost unconsciously.

Then it happened. In Copenhagen while on a business trip, I happened to be in a downtown pub. Though alone I was not particularly lonely ... just drinking a beer and thinking of my next day's schedule. A younger blonde rather handsome man sat down next to me. He smiled. I smiled in return. He moved closer toward me. I was confused thinking I had given him the wrong impression. He moved closer to me and rubbed his thigh against mine. I offered no resistance. We left. And the next phase of my journey began.

My first reaction to my experience was elation. Elation in the sense that this experience had added a new dimension to my sexual experience. I knew that sex with men had actually captivated me. It was the sexual activity rather than the attraction to men at this stage that had me captive. It then dawned on me that the activity was homosexual in the eyes of the majority culture. And where did I fit in the subculture of top and bottom men or dominant and submissive men? I avoided both quandaries for five years by asserting my heterosexuality to myself. I reasoned that since I was being serviced

# Life Story

by homosexuals that did not make me homosexual per se. This was a coping rationalisation since I did not want to come out to anyone, including myself, that I might be homosexual. A wise gay friend of our family said that I could find partners for anonymous sex at the local bath house on Monday lunchtime. He intimated that men who had not made out on the weekend would be eager to do so on Monday. He also indicated this was the favoured time of married men to indulge their fantasies. The word bisexual was not in general usage, and I could not be homosexual since I was neither feminine in appearance or behaviour. This myth sustained me during this first five year period.

Since anal sex did not appeal to me with either sex, I then considered myself neither top or bottom. Gradually however I became physically attracted and really turned on by men I considered attractive. At the same time I was still sexually intimate with my wife. In fact our sexual intimacy increased as I learned how to enhance my own sexual pleasure. I also learned the subtleties of oral sex with both sexes. My male contacts during this period were totally anonymous.

Gradually all of sexuality came out of the closet in our society. After Stonewall, single gay men did not want to be used by married men who refused to acknowledge their sexuality. In my travels I learned the language of eye contact and entendre that communicated the sexual desires of the other person. The frequency of my male contact grew until the early 1980s when the AIDS epidemic surfaced. I would tremble at reading the initial news articles since initially the manner of transmission was unknown. The pressure to be tested was overwhelming. I submitted to anonymous testing.

The results of the test were negative. I heaved a great sigh of relief ... At this time I was certain that I had not infected my wife. I could no longer hide my sexual orientation from her. I had started drinking heavily as a result of living in the underground world of inbetween. She reacted. She felt my change in orientation was a result of her sexual inadequacy. I assured her that was not the case. She needed time to digest the news. Her second response was a sense of grief. She grieved the loss of being one half of a married couple ... and now simply a partner. At the same time I was undergoing the transition into retirement. I was not handling retirement well. I also offered to go into a sexual addiction 12 step group to cope with my sexuality during this period. She recognised the concrete steps I was taking and we remained together. In the group I met other men facing the same problem of coming out and staying within a relationship. I concluded that my basic emotional problems stemmed from deep seated angers.

I was encouraged by fellow group members to undergo therapy which I did. My wife hoped that therapy would change my orientation back to heterosexual. I devoted a year and a half to therapy; I went every two weeks. It was a great experience. My anger disappeared. I felt healed. I felt whole. I felt energised. I also was still bisexual however. After each therapy session, I would come home and my wife and I would discuss for several hours what had taken place. She gained confidence in the process. I suggested she talk to a therapist as a friend and counsellor during this period. My therapist recommended a lady therapist for her. Her therapist was skilled in helping her through this transition and helping her adjust to the idea of a bisexual husband. She discussed boundaries and behaviours. She focussed on expectations and primacy of relationships. We were asked by both therapists to model a separation and see how we would feel and what our sense of loss would be. We did. It was a risk. We did not wish to give up our relationship.

During this time the AIDS epidemic had reached siege proportions in our community. The conservative right were talking about quarantining persons who were HIV+. As a symbolic way of "coming out", I volunteered for the local AIDS self-empowerment group. In this way I could be Bi in my volunteer activities. Since I had experience in management, I was helpful in the bureaucracy of the group. Writing by-laws, planning kitchens, doing a religious dedication, making pies, and picking up prescriptions. Each Sunday night we had a meditation and spirituality group that met ... about nine diagnosed and three of us non-diagnosed. At check-in each would tell of their week ... their anxieties ... their pain ... and their fear of death alone. I felt affirmed, honoured, to be there. But that is another story altogether.

The most painful part of this experience was falling in love with a man for whom I was caregiver. He wanted me to be on hand 24 hours a day. I could not because of my primary commitment to my wife. He fired me as caregiver. I was heartbroken ... I recovered. He was fortunate to find a loving caring man who cared for him as he wanted ... however I was with him at the time of his death to console his caregiver who replaced me. It is difficult to write this as I cry each time I think of him as he is still very special in my memory.

In 1992, I left the AIDS project. I had burned out. I am not an emotional giant. It was time for a new, less demanding challenge. Currently I am active in organisations dealing with homophobia. I have a close male friend who has left a long marriage and a love relationship with another man. We enjoy one another and give each other space which we both need. I am not out to my children at the

# Life Story

request of my wife and also because of the horror stories that I have heard from other fathers about rejection from their sons.

When I first acknowledged my gay side, I was angry. Why me? At this time in my life, I affirm it as it has allowed me to meet and understand many wonderful persons and to share the lives of some very courageous men that I might not have otherwise known. My anger has moved to joy. But underneath it all is the dynamic of change. Yes I am still alive ... and who knows what tomorrow will bring?

# Chapter 5

# MARDI GRAS: An Old-Fashioned Love Story

**Maria Pallotta-Chiarolli**

*for Alan and Naomi*

Mardi Gras.

She wears a short bright dress and high heels. He wears a white t-shirt and black bike pants. She looks pretty. He has the crew-cut clean look. Standard uniforms. She is straight straight. He is gay, but ...

It's their first Mardi Gras. They hadn't intended to spend it together.

Months earlier, the first time he saw her, he said, "Oh no" as he groaned. She said, "He's gorgeous, but he's gay" and at that point was still able to file him in an archive in her heart, like she did with many of the gorgeous gay boys.

Sydney, Mardi Gras. A place and time of exposures and revelations. Where masks of propriety and social conventions drop to the bottom of the Harbour. Where irrational regulations are queried. Where party masks and costumes create illusions through which the real illusions are exposed.

What they had kept safely locked away for months, moulded into innocent and manageable shapes by the unquestioning of assumptions

# Mardi Gras

and categories, comes completely undone as the music pounds, and the laserlights pierce the dancing bodies.

Her delicious body dances in front of him. Her eyes come up to meet his and sear him so that he needs oxygen in the heat, in the dance-floor sauna of sweating bodies. He can only look away, and fill his lungs with the Amyl, the smoke and the body colognes wafting around them. He tries to feel the same erotic energy for the sexy men dancing around him. But he can no longer block out the painful thought: he has fallen in love with HER.

He had been so comfortable for such a long time. Sometimes, if asked, he would say he was bisexual. But when he was with a man, this was overlooked. He fitted in. His first love had been a woman. She was black. As a teenager, he had not had the strength to challenge the racism. The relationship collapsed. From then on, he was gay. It was a lesser rebellion. He had a couple of lapses now and again. But only because the women initiated it, and it flattered him, ... and it felt good, actually. He had stabilised soon after, presenting a gay front with just the odd sideways glance at a woman or the quickening pulse to control.

We are simply dancing, she reminds herself. Simply dancing ... his firm thighs in bicycle shorts, the sweat shining on his arms. Simply dancing ... until too many times his eyes on her, drinking parts of her in, and her own eyes playing hide-and-seek with his mouth, his shoulders, his crotch. Simply dancing ... her lungs gasping for oxygen so she can keep some control.

"What's happening here?" she thinks in confusion. "He's gay and I'm heading for heartache. After years of faghag expertise, how could this happen to me?" She had always enjoyed the flirtation with him because it meant nothing to him. She'd say things like, "What could make you turn heterosexual?" He'd say, "Your legs" and just for a second ... but then they'd laugh. She couldn't take him seriously. And that had become more and more painful. She realised she was falling in love with HIM.

They dance, his fingertips touching her waist, pulling her closer ... or did she push forward? They sway together.

And the masks slide off their wet bodies.

They cling in stillness, while the revellers swarm around them. They are both part of and apart from them.

They make some attempts to retrieve the masks. She thinks, "He is gay, isn't he? I'm not going to be his experiment with hetsex." He thinks, "Why her when I'm surrounded by these male hunks? Is this her idea of kinky sex?" They stare at each other with suspicion. They pull apart and then feel themselves melting into each other.

She shakes her head slowly. "We can't," she says. "I know," he says. Not much conviction in their voices.

She's frustrated. He's supposed to be reliable company. He's frustrated. He's finally at a Mardi Gras and all he wants to do is hold this woman.

"Let's go," he says and they make their way out of the hall. She remembers how they'd entered. A man in leather, backside firm and tanned, had passed by them, mesmerising them. They had caught the lust in each other's eyes. "It's tempting," she'd said. "I have a far better chance at him than you," he'd teased. "You never know," she'd remarked, but agreed with him nevertheless. They had laughed and begun to dance.

In the taxi on the way home, as she's about to get out, he whispers, "I love you". She slams the door.

He calls out, "I'll be thinking of you", and she runs across the road and only looks back when she thinks the taxi's gone. But he's waving. She waves too, whispers goodbye, and blows him a kiss.

This is the end, she decides, as she takes the lift to her room. Short and sweet. He will regret Mardi Gras tomorrow. He will feel uncomfortable next time he sees her. It was all in the heat of the moment. He is now wondering how on earth he could have felt whatever he felt for a woman, and this plain mediocre naive woman in particular. She will have to readjust her mask, and pretend it was all a mistake for her too.

In the taxi, he worries that her wave and that kiss are rather too definite. She knows how he really feels. That what was said was from his heart. Will she still feel the same? Will she ever want to at least talk about this? He feels so confused, and yet things have never seemed clearer.

Nothing will happen. It cannot. In their separate rooms, as they struggle to get some sleep while the new day's sun slices through the post-Mardi Gras haze, they feel both relieved and sad at this thought.

All they know for sure is how they feel – the love, the joy, the breathtaking freedom of having it all said and unmasked. And the sadness, the pain, the trap that they're in now that it's all been said and unmasked.

Where do they go from here? Their labels and neat categories have collapsed. Their worlds have lost definite boundaries, and yet this borderlessness feels so refreshing, so alive. As if they have clawed out of coffins and through six feet of soil.

Mardi Gras 29

Mardi Gras.

She wears a black high-cut body-suit. He wears bright purple bike pants and bare chest. Her hair is in an intricate formation. He is growing his. She is not-so-straight straight. He is bisexual. They enjoy the Mardi Gras together.

It's been a strange, painful, traumatic year. In trying to be true to their new unfixed selves, they have hurt those they love and been hurt in return. They've done things, said things, made decisions, taken risks they never thought they would. That's what happens when the labels and categories no longer fit. There's few other role models.

But they're here again at Mardi Gras, stronger together than last year. The struggle is still on, still pieces to put together in a jigsaw puzzle that is far more flexible and fluid than the socially constructed one they left behind. But just for tonight, they want to celebrate the good times they've had, they want to be themselves hoping those selves together don't matter.

Because they have discovered their two selves together do matter so much, not only in straight land where their relationship can't be pinned to a wall, neatly labeled and conveniently ignored. It also matters in their Oxford Street neighbourhood amongst the so-called radical who can become conservative and oppressive. Oxford Street is not such a haven anymore. There are less smiles, more blatant stares.

On the night at an HIV political rally, one of the prominent HIV-positive speakers, an old friend, has just given a stirring speech on the need to end discrimination, on the need to let people love whom they choose and release the heterosexist stranglehold. They move forward to congratulate him. He doesn't have anything to say to her now, and only this to sneer at him, "So, have you stopped sleeping with women yet?"

Bouncers at the doors of gay venues are puzzled for months. "Do you realize this is a gay place?" "I'm bi and my girlfriend-" and they reluctantly let them in with a look of almost parental disapproval. Or- "Sorry, no straights tonight." Or- "It's GAY men only." Or suddenly they're paying double what the two gay guys in front of them paid. His bisexuality could only be overlooked when with a man.

He sits at a supposedly with-it cafe. The men at the next table converse: "Here he is again. He holds her hand pretending to be straight but when she's not around, he's here hoping to score." She rages at the stereotypes they have of her. They can only slot her into one of two possible frames – the naive duped woman, or the conniving woman attempting to convert a gay man into straight. They don't seem to be able to transcend these soap opera scenarios.

In a gay sex-shop back-room: "He hangs around gay places for a thrill but he's just a naughty straight boy." Or- "He's only here to perve, but he never takes up the offers. She's got him well-trained". Should he explain? "I've got the right to say no as much as I've got the right to say yes."

They've often sat in gay places and watched other male-female couples for clues. Are they bi, straight, good friends, who knows? Should it matter?

Mardi Gras.

She is wearing black velvet short shorts, a bustierre, and suspenders with fish-nets. He wears a leather and chain harness and leather short shorts. Her hair is wild. His is sleeked back into a ponytail. She is queer-straight. He is bisexual. At the Parade and at the dance, people stare. They want to figure it out. Put them in a neat box. Is he gay? Is he straight? Are they together? Are they friends? Is she a femme dyke? Is she a post-op transsexual success story? Is he a leather man? What on earth is she then? His SM slave?

They enjoy the Mardi Gras together. Their lives and other relationships have regained much balance. There is much healing, forgiveness, solid friendships on steady ground, and their regrets, mistakes and angers are somehow easier to live with.

Their "mixed marriage", as they call it, is now old news. They have very accepting close friends, while others politely tolerate, and still others hover in the dark shadows and wait for disaster so they can pounce. Their closet has swinging doors on it. Some people will probably never be told, others will be eased into it gradually, and still others know-and-do-not-want-to-know-and-so-pretend-they-do-not-know-because-they-don't-know-what-to-do-if-they-say-they-do-know. Others have become armchair anthropologists researching this peculiar social phenomena.

The gossip has died down in their Oxford Street neighbourhood. They're like pieces of furniture that you can't axe for firewood, you can't feel comfortable with, and you feel funny having them around, but somehow they're there and actually would be missed if they were thrown out. And you know, they're quite nice pieces of furniture anyway. Indeed, many younger immigrants to these blocks don't really care. Everyone's queer and you can't tell who's who anymore. And identity politics can become too confining.

"A mixed cultural, mixed gender marriage". They compare notes on split ends and hair dyes. He wears her mascara on special nights out and flutters the eyelashes at all the good-looking boys who hear him say how much he loves her. She wears his leather shorts, experiments with his leather and chain harness, and dreams about fulfilling her big fantasy, being behind one of those tough sexy-looking dykes on bikes in a future Mardi Gras. He has the same fantasy.

He won the best-dressed award at a gay fancy-dress event by wearing her old school uniform, replete with straw hat and fish-net stockings. They went as schoolgirl buddies which they sometimes feel they are as they giggle and stir about the way their "rebellion" confounds their overseers. Their conversations give away the fact that this is not a straight couple. But the way they are together means neither of them are gay. They're best friends and they're in love, but don't own a rulebook.

He says, "I don't know whether to be jealous when a man comes onto you because he's chatting up the person I love or because he's not coming onto me." She laughs and says, "Be both and neither."

He says: "If we break up, I'll be hunting along Oxford Street, looking for another woman to fuck me." She says: "I hope you find her and are happy with her." And she loves him too much not to mean it.

He says: "I really like him. Almost began wanting to get to know him a little better but then he said he hates bisexual men." She says: "Don't worry, there'll be someone else. That attitude is on its way out."

He says: "I'm monogamous with you because I want to be." She says: "That's OK. You might change your mind tomorrow."

She says: "I wish I was bisexual too." He says: "You're bisexual by marriage. Anyway, if you can say that, then you are. You can be a bisexual virgin just like a straight or gay virgin."

One day he slides a ring onto her finger. "Like a nice straight boy," he says and then she reads what he's written in the card: 'Don't marry me forever. This is not a proposal."

They dream of an old age when they'll stroll down Oxford Street together and everyone is just sexual with no prefixes and creating whatever form of love they need. They'll remember the days they were breaking the rules of both the rulers and the rebels. They'll remember the hurt they caused and the hurt they bore. Time might have brought new questions of each other, new expectations from each other, as they glided and stumbled along between being "friends" and "lovers". But if they've called it quits before then, nothing will make them regret or forget the power and beauty of what they had.

# Chapter 6

# Group Sex

**Alison Rowan**[1]

Picture the scene – two blonde, busty women, overcome by frustration, falling all over each other in a steamy but basically unorgasmic love scene. Suddenly the door opens – her husband is home early. "Oh Frank! just when we could use a nice juicy cock!" (I'm not joking, I actually read that line somewhere!)

The reality is fortunately rather different, but all too often we allow these dishonest pictures of our lives to put us off what would otherwise be pleasurable adventures. It pains me to think how long it took me to admit that my very first sexual encounter with a woman was as part of a threesome with my straight boyfriend. At the time I was having a hard enough time fitting in without putting off the few bi-friendly women I knew!

Since then I've enjoyed threesomes and foursomes of many different moods and combinations, from a long term arrangement with my boyfriend and a female lover, to a one night adventure with three lovers and a riding crop. Far from the image of two women being used voyeuristically by a man, my all time favourite was probably the first time I saw two *men* making love. I had begun to get jealous of my boyfriend's first male lover, and seeing them together and participating was a wonderful antidote and very beautiful to watch.

Not a lot has been written about group sex, especially in bisexual publications where we are perhaps still a little unsure of ourselves or too jealous of the little space we that we have to spend any of it

---

[1] This article previously appeared in *Bifrost*

on what has to be one of the major bisexual stereotypes. The fact is, though, that some bisexuals *do* do group sex (and probably a lot more would like to), and we are being let down by the available literature, which, even when it doesn't fall for the "men and women in lurve" myth, allows precious little time for sex as an expression of friendship and adventure. An exception to this for me was The Joy of Sex and More Joy of Sex (the earlier editions and not the "post-AIDS" expurgated editions). Although some of the comments jar when I re-read them now, their acceptance of bisexuality and down-to-earth advice about group sex was very helpful to me at the time.

One comment that stays with me is about how *educational* a group sex scene can be. After all, not even all that many sexologists have actually seen a couple, of whichever genders, having sex. It is very different to watch than to participate, and it can be particularly fascinating to watch two people of the other sex together. It is easy to feel guilty about this when "voyeur" is considered an insult, but it is a natural part of any group scene, and having a break while you get gently turned on and intrigued by watching other people is entirely different to the picture of the frustrated male voyeur who can't wait to dive to the "rescue" with his cock!

It is very hard to advise on how to conduct a group scene. In "Sapphistry" Pat Califia suggests that a group of women get together to negotiate before anything gets started. This may be advisable, but it has never happened that way with me. What is more likely to happen is that two (or more) people decide they would really like to get a third person to bed. This can be a little unfair on the third party, so don't forget that people are generally more able to express their feelings one-to-one. It may seem a little clumsy taking turns to go to the toilet or make coffee while the other two have a quick chat, but its better than getting someone into a scene that they don't really want.

Every experience of group sex will be different (another way in which real life differs from the porn films), but there are a few basic ground rules and ideas that can make it go more smoothly. The first is to make enough time and space for what you want to do. Group sex tends to take longer than "ordinary" sex, after all once you've got that person to bed you want to make the most of it, and you need to allow time for people to get over their embarrassment and get turned on. Space is also important, although I have managed a threesome half in and half out of a 2' 6" bunk bed I wouldn't recommend it. Don't be put off if you don't have a mansion with six foot beds, though – cushions or mattresses on the floor are just as good – and people *can* manage to make love in a much smaller space than they could all comfortably sleep in.

The other major ground rule is about expectations. The more people are involved the less chance there is of all of them getting exactly what they want – so be flexible. Penetration is a particularly intimate experience, and not everyone will want it. If you do have a willing partner it might be polite to ask the others if they mind, as it can take you away from the action a bit and seem exclusive. And don't expect multiway simultaneous orgasms – group sex is often a more relaxed experience than sex in a couple.

There's not a lot more to say, except that it is perfectly acceptable to spend the first half of the evening saying "are we really doing this?". The people in the porn films wouldn't dare let themselves be caught giggling – but we know better than that ...

# Chapter 7

# Life Story

**Becca**

I am 21, heterosexual, a psychology major at Carnegie Mellon University, which is about 70% male, and an officer in a social organisation which is about 85% male. I share an apartment with two men with whom I'm not romantically/physically involved. All my close friends here are male, and of the old friends with whom I'm still in touch, I only feel close to one woman. I don't see the lack of female influence on my life as a problem, although sometimes I ponder whether it is a problem in some way and I just haven't noticed. I consider myself reasonably feminine (not a tomboy) but I just don't connect well with most women.

At the moment I'm recovering from a long-term relationship which was "open" all the way through, sometimes smoothly and sometimes not. The reason it ended was that Ian moved away, and we thought (probably correctly) that we couldn't maintain it long-distance. He's been gone almost two months now, and I still miss him, but in the last week or so I've started to see signs of recovery. I've been seeing Dan since May, except for the last two weeks Ian was in town, when we agreed not to see each other so I could spend a lot of time with Ian. At the moment I am seeing only Dan and not really looking for additional lovers but not ruling out the possibility. I haven't allowed Dan to replace Ian in the role of ever-present steady boyfriend; I think it's time for a break from that, and I'm enjoying my independence and beginning to have more of a sense of who I am as myself, rather than in relation to other people. Dan and I see each other mainly on weekends and spend varying amounts of time together, anything from going to a movie to spending 48 hours together as we did this past weekend. This isn't an arrangement I've really tried before, and it has its advantages. Yesterday I told him, for the first time, that I love him. His reaction was, "Wow, I don't know what to think." which seemed not to be a bad thing, and I wasn't hurt that he didn't reciprocate. I find it hard to believe in the traditional idea of romance, preferring to put the emphasis on what Ian called "the union of friendship and desire."

Looking back at my childhood, I can see things that may indicate I've been poly all along. I always had trouble imagining myself married, and when I played house with my best friend, she always pretended her husband was away on business, while I thought it was more interesting to be a single mom who went on dates with different strange characters. In grade school the assumption was that girls should pair off as best friends, and for a couple of those years it was considered disloyal to play with anyone other than your best friend, unless you were with a group. Although I managed to cope with this system, I resented the reduction of options and the quarrelling that happened when one of us wanted to do something and the other didn't. It seemed perfectly reasonable to me that I should have at least one friend who shared each of my interests, instead of trying to make my best friend enjoy all the same things I did.

This is much the way I feel about polyamory. Having multiple lovers makes as much sense to me as having multiple friends. It is unfair to expect one person to be everything to me, and it is unfair to myself to ignore one of my interests because my partner doesn't enjoy it.

I was a socially awkward kid and also had strict parents, so I didn't date at all until I was 16, and then my behaviour was different from the paradigm, not out of intentional rebellion but because I was doing what seemed reasonable to me. I'm from a small Oklahoma town where kids start "going together" in fifth grade (meaning they form pairs in which two people of opposite sexes speak to each other!) and start dating in seventh or eighth grade, *always* monogamously. Two people who go on a date are immediately assumed to be "going out" until they formally agree to stop. You are either in a couple or you aren't; there is no such thing as dating around. As a high school sophomore, I began attending parties with my group of friends (by then a mixed-sex group) at which parents were usually home but in another room, and the main activity was watching VCR movies in semi-darkness, which meant that the other main activity was covert sexual behaviour. Doing this as surreptitiously as possible was considered a matter of style. The unusual thing about my group, as compared to others in our school, was that most of us acted "single" and those who did form couples did so with someone else from the group. Once it became known that some of us were sexually active, our group was referred to by others as "the F.Y.F. Club," standing for "Fuck Your Friends." I still find it puzzling that anyone would think this is a bad thing; if the people you fuck are not your friends, who are they?! Anyway, although people meant it as a derogatory name, we adopted it as our own, enjoying the similarity to M.Y.F. and L.Y.F. (local church youth groups). I began letting guys drive me home from parties where I had aroused them, knowing that that meant we would park somewhere along the way. It was never assumed on either side that this constituted "going out."

I realized all along that I was acting in ways that, according to local popular belief, qualified me as a slut. This status was not my objective (satisfying sexual curiosity was), but I thought it was pretty cool. It was completely contrary to the image of me that most people at my school had, and consequently they tended to discard any information about my activities (which was not difficult to get, since my friends and I often discussed sex while eating lunch) and I never really got a Reputation. I lost my virginity to a male friend who called me one night and point-blank asked if I would like to have sex with him. We started as "fuckbuddies" and decided we were "going out" after about three months. He graduated a year ahead of me and joined the Army Reserve, so he was away a lot. We had an understanding that we could date other people at any time, but I didn't, largely because there was no one in that town who really interested me; I did fool around with friends from time to time.

In 1991 I started college and had a few short-lived, unfortunate monogamous relationships. In fact, part of the reason for the shortness and unfortunateness was the assumption of monogamy. For instance, in my first two days at college I met two attractive men, James and Shawn, who were both interested in me, but Shawn had a girlfriend back home. He and I had a long discussion in which he admitted he was just as strongly attracted to me as to his girlfriend but knew he couldn't have both of us at once. He asked me why this was true, why our society doesn't allow us to be with everyone we want. I realized then that I couldn't think of a good answer to that question. Oddly enough, that realization did not prompt me to question the paradigm. I simply began a relationship with James because he was available. Although James is a great guy and we had some good times together, I really wanted Shawn too, and so when Shawn's girlfriend broke up with him, I thought the right thing to do was to leave James for Shawn. Shawn then broke up with me after less than a week, and because I had treated James badly, I wound up with nobody at all.

In January 1992 I began dating Chris and "fell head over heels in love." This is the only time this has ever happened to me, and I still wonder if I was really feeling what I was supposed to or just deluding myself. If the latter, I did it pretty well. We adored each other completely, spent most of our free time together for a semester, were separated for a summer, and then fused ourselves together again. But ... in September 1992 we had a threesome with a friend (male, bi. Chris is straight) and I began to admit that I felt attracted to other men. I might have pushed that aside as a normal feeling I shouldn't act on, but a few weeks later, Chris "cheated on me" with another girl. We argued for a few more weeks and decided to open the relationship. We were successfully poly and happy in a few brief periods, arguing all the rest of the time until April 1993 when we broke up. The main point of contention was that Chris couldn't stand my being with other men, regardless of his own behaviour; also, due to the ratio here, he had trouble finding partners and felt left out. Immediately after the breakup I became involved with Ian. He and I did better at polyamory than Chris and I did, but we had many arguments also, mostly over the same points and also because Ian got in a rut sexually and was then upset when I found other men more exciting.

For the first three months I was with Ian, he was also dating a woman who lived in another city and visited him for several days every few weeks. She was upset by his refusal to be monogamous to her, so during her visits I was not allowed to see Ian at all, and she refused to meet me. I was upset by this but tolerated it, rationalising that I got to see Ian more often so it was okay for her to get his undivided attention when she was here. After each of her visits, Ian told me in considerable detail all the nice things she had done for him and how much he had enjoyed sex with her. For the most part, I didn't mind, although I did feel jealous when he made direct comparisons and said the other woman was better. After she broke up with him, he tried to attract other women, but nothing worked out. I think much of his jealousy about my other relationships was due to discouragement about his trouble finding other partners for himself, and I suspect we'd have been much happier if he had. I felt this way at the time, too, and encouraged him to find someone else, but because I know so few females, I wasn't able to "set him up" with anyone. Despite his jealousy, he was fairly tolerant until I got involved with Dan; he and Dan had been friends for years, and he took it as a betrayal on both our parts. Ian stopped speaking to Dan, tried to talk me out of seeing him, and insisted that I not talk about him. Had Ian stayed in town, I think my relationship with him would have ended anyway because we wouldn't have been able to resolve the argument over Dan.

Polyamory is the only issue on which I still feel adolescently confused. I spend a lot of time trying to figure out what I *need*, what I want if I can get it, how I can deal with this socially, and what this means for my future. I don't think I can ever be completely faithful to one man for more than a year at a stretch, and I don't think I should have to be, but I also want, eventually, a stable household and a child, and I'm not sure how I'm going to work that out. I have "come out" only to my brother, one cousin, and a poly uncle who is sort of a role model. I am not sure how my parents would react to this or when or how I should tell them. Also, polyamory is fairly acceptable here at college, especially in my social group, but I worry about feeling alone in the "real world."

When I first tried polyamory I was not certain that it was right for me, but despite the problems I've encountered, with experience and introspection I've decided this is the only way I can live happily. I don't feel right about a situation in which I am completely dependent on someone for my emotional well-being and he is completely dependent on me; I feel it is much better for people to depend on each other in a sort of web. I think polyamory is a component of sexuality: I am polyamorously heterosexual, and I can't change either part of that. Limiting myself to one person, especially pledging lifelong faithfulness to one person, seems no more natural to me, for me, than having sex with a woman. Although I often feel social pressure to be monogamous and sometimes feel persecuted when it seems that nobody understands my viewpoint, I think I have a right to express my love for multiple people. The more love I give, the more I get in return.

# Chapter 8

# Choosing Not to Choose: Beyond Monogamy, Beyond Duality

Maria Pallotta-Chiarolli, Faculty of Social Science, University of Technology, Sydney, Australia.

## Foreword

This article is a result of several years of questions and observations, and my associations and discussions with many people of diverse ethnic, sexual and marital lifestyles living in responsible nonmonogamous relationships. It presents part of the theories and empirical material I will be exploring in my Ph.D. studies. Thus, it is very much a skeletal framework. The names and some other identifying features of the people participating in my study have been altered for confidentiality.

Upon first reading, the seven personal life stories may appear too positive, too idealistic. Closer reading will reveal the social pressures and personal dilemmas that the individuals concerned experienced and/or are still experiencing. I believe it is important to present successful examples of negotiated multipartner relationships to begin addressing the stereotypes and negative constructions in the mainstream media, literature, and psychological/sociological analyses.

# 8.1 Introduction

*I'm simply trying to live a
both/and life in an either/or
world (Tom Robinson, quoted by Bennett, 1992 : 205).*

*Two roads diverged in a yellow wood
and I, I took both (Gary North, in Geller, 1990 : 8).*

This article examines how individuals who are in responsible nonmonogamous relationships locate themselves or are constructed as being located within, outside, on the borders, or "slipping between the cracks" of social and cultural groups and established discourses. They find themselves often challenging and being challenged by the discourses and political ideologies of both powerful central and power-challenging marginal groups.

As Gibian writes about the "Almighty Power of Opposition", "our entire Western system of thought is based on binary opposition; we define by comparison, by what things are not ... [and by] entities that exclude each other" (1992:5). She cites Derrida's critique of the use of polarities as containing a hierarchy in which the second term in the pair is negative and undesirable, as in man/woman, heterosexuality/homosexuality, monogamous/nonmonogamous. Bennett (1992) defines this as "hierarchical dualism", which favours exclusion and domination, ignorance and dogmatism.

> It has obscured and marginalised the connectedness between diverse beings, the equal value-in-themselves of all beings, and the possibility for personal fluidity and transformation (1992:210).

Any concept of ambiguity as positive and enriching, as presented through the shifting identities and relationships in Rita Mae Brown's **Bingo**, is denigrated. As Nickie, the female narrator states toward the beginning of the novel,

> My parents didn't raise me to have relationships with married people but my parents didn't take into account the slim pickings in Runnymede, especially if one is gay. Which brings me to what appears to be a flaming contradiction. What was I doing in bed with Jackson Frost? Having a good time. (1988:45).

Her lover is married to her best friend, Regina. They know Nickie is a lesbian and Jackson relies on her understanding of marginality to point out his dilemma: "I'm in love with two women at the same time.

In our society there's no more room for me than there is for the gay person" (1988:173). When she finds out she is pregnant to Jackson, Nickie makes the painful choice of ending their relationship, only to find that Mr Pierre, the town's gay hairdresser, wants to marry her. He explains:

> "My life has never been the same since Bob died. For a while there I lost the reason to live ... People don't have to sleep together to be a family. They only have to love one another and I already love you." "I love you too. I don't think I'm going to be much of a wife," I said quietly. ... "I know, darling. I'll be a better wife than you will." (1988:255).

Just before the wedding, Regina tells Nickie she knows about her relationship and love for Jackson and that the baby is his:

> "I'm not really hurt by the fact you slept with Jack. I'm hurt by the fact that you didn't tell me ... we could have worked it out ... I don't believe love is a controlled substance. You can't outlaw it or confine it within the bonds of matrimony. It wasn't as if you stole anything from me. I don't own him. I don't want to own him" (1988:279-280).

The friendship between the two women becomes even stronger. When the twins are born, Jack and Regina visit "if not once a day, then every day" (1988:288) and equal co-parenting is set up between Nickie's newspaper office and Mr Pierre's hairdressing salon. Mr Pierre also tells Nickie about a woman who has a crush on her. What Nickie will do about this isn't decided in the novel for it really doesn't matter.

Sensationalised stereotypes about nonmonogamous relationships conspire with silence about diverse realities to perpetuate ignorance, self-and-other doubt and self-and-other hatred. Stories such as the above reveal the greater complexities and options.

Multiple partnerships need not mean conflict between lifelong monogamy and dishonest, secretive nonmonogamy; nor the synthesis of the two polarities of marital monogamy and so-called "promiscuity" as in serial monogamy; but an actual invention of new meaning or transcendence into new relationship models such as multipartnering. Instead of meaning deriving from dualistic coercions, meaning derives from multiple options where everything exists in wholeness in relation to everything else.

The concept of "deviance" is also based on "hierarchical dualism" and implies social ascription and categorisation. In his study of deviance-designation of women, Schur cites the work of Becker (1963):

social groups create deviance by making the rules whose infraction constitutes deviance, and by applying these rules to particular people and labelling them as outsiders. ... [therefore] deviance is not a quality of the act the person commits, but rather a consequence of the application by others of rules and sanctions to an "offender" (1983:5).

Deviance lies in the "eye of the beholder". Beholding is affected by the beholder's social experiences and positions. Schur outlined three results of labelling deviance which are relevant to the labelling of persons of diverse ethnic, sexual and "alternative", as in responsible nonmonogamous, lifestyles. First, their deviance becomes their "master status". In other words, they are "seen", identified and responded to solely or mainly in terms of that deviant status. Furthermore, once this categorical label is applied, people tend to impute to the individual various "auxiliary traits" or stereotypes they believe to be "characteristic of anyone bearing the label". Second, individuals in the devalued category are thought of as comprising a "unitary or homogeneous type". Schur calls this "maintaining consistency": "they" are a problem; "they" are all alike; "they" are recognisable as such. Selective inattention will occur where whatever contradicts the stereotype will not be noticed. Third, "objectification" occurs where a person becomes nothing but "their membership in the stigma-laden category" (1983:24-30). Schur believes that efforts at deviance-designation usually rests on a powerful group's perception of the threat posed by the "deviants". For example, responsible nonmonogamists defy and contradict dominant constructions of history, culture, science and other so-called truths and ideologies. They are "dangerous evidence that recorded knowledge is inaccurate" (Farley, 1985:269). They must be denied, "the unthinkable alternative, the nonchoice" in order to validate what is socio-culturally and politically constructed to be the only choice or alternative. They must be "wrong, so the other can be right; to be bad, so the other can be good; to be unnatural, so the other can be natural" (1985: 270).

In struggling to achieve socio-political power and cultural status, power-challenging groups such as gay activists and feminists, and indeed nonmonogamists who deride persons who choose monogamous relationships, may emulate the control/conformity and deviance-designating systems of their oppressors, thus also becoming both oppressed and oppressive. Gibian quotes from Meg Christian's **From The Heart**:

> Where are we going when our principles start to stunt our growing? ... where is our freedom when we've broken old

chains just to make new ones? (1992:3).

Meekosha and Pettman (1990) see the need to move beyond "category politics" by beginning with a conscious recognition of the many sites of power and oppression, and their commonalities and overlaps. The language of "oppression, solidarity and community need both deconstructing and tightening" (1990:14). A minority group or community identity can provide security and support, and a location to plan and implement strategies of resistance to mainstream power. However, in its need to create a united, solid front against the external enemy, a minority community can devise its own systems of censorship and stricture of differences. Rigid conformity and uniformity become internally coercive as a means of resisting external social coercion (Udis-Kessler, 1990; Pallotta-Chiarolli, 1993).

In dealing with the dichotomies of being either the "outsider" or "insider", personal identity and degrees of "insider/outsider" status are determined in at least one of three ways: first, experiencing conflict between the polarities resulting in an either/or choice or coerced decision (either get married and try to live a heterosexual monogamous lifestyle or resist marriage altogether); second, negotiating and synthesising elements of both polarities resulting in a location along a continuum between the two binaries (such as serial monogamists); and third, transcending the polarities to construct an identity that is multiple, fluid, beyond binaries and dualities (such as married and unmarried nonmonogamists of varying sexualities).

Throughout the process of determining one's identities and choices within a range of relationship models, the significance of three intersecting forces become apparent: first, social ascription or the labels and categories imposed on oneself by the outside wider society; second, community acknowledgement (both positive and negative) being the labels and categories one's significant others affirm or disapprove; and third, personal agency, or the individual selecting and determining necessary or desired labels from the constructions available, or attempting to devise an alternative model for oneself. For example, in Robert Heinlein's novel, **To Sail Beyond The Sunset**, Briney and Maureen, a non-monogamous married couple, carry out their own form of resistance and self-definition against the surrounding conventions:

> Briney and I did not work out all our rules for sex and love and marriage too easily. We were trying to do two things at once: create a whole new system of just conduct in marriage – a code that any civilised society would have taught us as children – and simultaneously create an arbitrary and utterly pragmatic set of rules for public

conduct to protect us from Bible-belt arbiters of morals and conduct. We were not missionaries trying to convert Mrs Grundy to our way of thinking; we simply wanted to hold up a mask so that she would never suspect that we did not agree with her way of thinking. In a society in which it is a moral offence to be different from your neighbours your only escape is never to let them find out (1987: 124).

In the post-structuralist thinking of the late eighties and early nineties, our society has become increasingly pluralist so that we are all exposed to a myriad of cultures, religions, traditions and lifestyle options. Angelico discusses how a coherent set of meanings can emerge from several diverging sources of reality. A "clarification process" occurs where meanings are identified, irrelevant meanings are discarded, meanings considered to be of value are retained, and new meanings are incorporated. There are many advantages to this multiplicity of identities and models such as "exposure to a broader range of possibilities" which provide more "options to choose". Also, "potentially conflicting situations can be a stimulus for self challenge and growth" rather than necessarily being a "liability" (1989:9). As many of the non-monogamists who I spoke with say, the transition to nonmonogamy usually involved painful situations.

Society would eventually comprise individuals with a "pluralistic personality". People would not be trapped in the duality of what they had inherited and what the dominant group wished to enforce, or indeed any single set of perceptions, but would learn to see things in the many ways possible; "even if we do not fully embrace" them, "we see clearly the valid points which lead others to choose differently". Novak calls the resultant society the "City of Humans" (1982:6). Individuals would always be represented as multifaceted and occupying varying positions. The reality of complex identities and the crossing of category boundaries needs to be further acknowledged in social theory in order to move beyond or transcend the false construction of homogeneities and universalities (Pallotta-Chiarolli, 1991, 1992, 1993, 1994).

# 8.2 Bisexuality and Multiple Relationships

Individuals who identify as bisexual often find themselves "excluded and absent" in both the power-challenging gay and lesbian groups and the powerful heterosexist wider society (see Wittstock, 1990; Himelhoch, 1990). Mass culture, history and social sciences have left bisexuals hidden among heterosexuals and homosexuals.

> To maintain the status quo, it is important that people can be classed categorically as either hetero- or homosexual. Hence bisexuality is invisibilised (George, 1991:2).

It also challenges the heterosexist power structure as it makes everyone difficult to control through neat classification and detachment. The so-called "deviants" are not easily compartmentalised into a controllable arena; they are within and part of the "normal" group.

*Sandra, Justin, Rebecca*

For three years, Sandra, a bisexual woman from Brisbane, Queensland, lived with Justin, a heterosexual man, and Rebecca, a bisexual woman. They were in their mid-twenties. Originally, Sandra met Rebecca at a lesbian event and the two of them found themselves "pretending to be pure dykes". After a couple of months, as they realised the intensity of their emotional as well as sexual feelings for each other, they both decided to "tell the truth". Rebecca "confessed" she was in love with a "straight boy" who knew about her love for Sandra. Sandra "confessed" she was actually bisexual and did not feel threatened by Rebecca's relationship with Justin. Over the next few months, the three began to see more of each other as a threesome, and Sandra and Justin realised they felt very strongly about each other as well.

The next step was to live together and this relationship lasted for three years. During that time, their relationship witnessed many shifts in imposed labels by significant others. "Some friends became enemies", especially some lesbian friends who believed Justin was exploiting both women. Family members who had accepted the "alternative sexuality" could not accept the "abnormal lifestyle". Going out together as a threesome required courage to be open or depending on the context, one of them would be the "close friend". This external pressure was the main factor of the break-up of the relationship.

Today, Sandra acknowledges that relationship as being the most "fulfilling, loving time" in her life. However, the "pressures of the closet" created divisions and sadnesses and she moved out. A few months later, Justin and Rebecca also broke up. Somehow, disrupting the "excellence of our three-way relationship left them feeling that their two-way one lacked something. But we're all friends now." Sandra would definitely consider a similar relationship but without any member having a "closet". "It's no big deal, really. Monogamous and non-monogamous relationships can be great. I know. I've had both."

*Paul, Alison, Matthew*

Paul and Alison have lived together in Sydney, New South Wales for almost all of their forty married years. Throughout most of those years, Paul was openly having relationships with men. "I've always loved Alison. We have three children. Well, they're adults now and one of my daughters is a lesbian. Being a grandfather is just marvellous. So, there's that whole family thing which I truly wanted. And yes, I did have very important relationships with men along the way but somehow they never stood the test of time or of love as with Alison. Long ago, Alison and I decided that if ever I should wish to move out and live with a man and see her and the children as well, I could do that. But it never happened until now. For the last few months, I've actually moved in with Matthew because even though I'm old, I've suddenly found the man I want to live with. But Alison and I see each other everyday and I see my family too. They're all very accepting. I think we raised them to understand the special love their mother and I always had for each other and they trusted us to never do anything that would hurt them or each other. Alison has been monogamous all these years. That's the way she is, she says. She's not a doormat. An amazing woman, very strong and independent. She always had her own professional life, great confidence in herself. A feminist even before feminism became a household word. She demanded my honesty, my love, my equal parenting and domestic sharing, and a good sexual, affectionate relationship but sexual ownership was something she worried about only for a few months after I began my first relationship with a man, and then she realised she was worrying because society said she should. The only other time she started worrying again was when the AIDS crisis arrived in Australia. We worked that out. Her basic attitude is that my bisexuality must be one of the components that make me the man she fell deeply in love with when we were in our early twenties and there was no way she was going to leave me unless she was unhappy with me. The hardest part of our marriage was the secrecy with work colleagues and family, and the agonies and hurts we caused and had to face when some loved ones found out along the way but as we got older we got tougher and braver. That's a good thing about aging. You stop worrying about being judged. You get freer. And along the way, we've got stronger as we've watched other so-called "normal, natural" marriages crumble or just dry up, especially the relationships of some of our knockers. And I got stronger in standing up to these gay activist types who couldn't figure out why I didn't leave her and lead a "normal" gay life. Come to think of it, that word gets used by everyone to knock someone else!

Alison has got to know some of my male lovers as friends. But she
thinks Matthew's the best. In fact, she encouraged me to try living
with him. 'You deserve to try it, Paul, after all these years. Don't
die without taking that opportunity. I'll still be here. Plus you know
I can take care of myself.' That's love, really. Wanting the best for
someone you love."

From both sides, "sleeping with the enemy" can be identified as
problematic and the bisexual person may be internalising these messages of confusion, betrayal, disorder, immaturity and "a stage in
working through false consciousness before finally arriving at one's
true [fixed] sexual orientation ... people who can't make up their
minds, or who are afraid to" (Weise 1992:ix). Thus, being bisexual
can be a major conflict in life, torn between the demands of the heterosexual and homosexual groups and often living with what Brewer
calls a "two-way closet" in denying aspects of oneself that prevent the
smooth assimilation into either sexuality group (1991:140).

Weise writes about bisexual women moving between the polarities
of lesbian or heterosexual,

> she rearranged her interior landscape of desire to conform
> to outside pressure, which she internalised to the extent
> that the pressure didn't feel like it was on the outside
> at all, but coming only from inside of her. She felt as
> if there were only two possibilities, so she had to fit all
> her feelings and desires into the narrow confines given
> her, like Cinderella's step-sisters cutting off their toes and
> heels to get the glass slipper to fit (1992:x-xi).

Golden (1987) presents examples of how women confront the need to
fit the glass slipper of heterosexuality or homosexuality by reinterpreting past experience of the "other" sexuality as "unreal" or deficient,
thus having resolved the conflict by highlighting one group as inferior,
the other superior in the binary opposition of the deficit model.

Bisexuality challenges many of the assumptions of our society: the
duality of gender; the necessity of bipolar relationships; the demand
for either/or sexualities; and monogamy as the only valid relationship model. A bisexual-feminist perspective embraces the reality that
sexuality can be a fluid and changeable part of being human, rejecting the dichotomisation of politics and desire, and "confronting culturally prescribed notions of duality and conflict" (Weise,1992: xi).
Even Kinsey's continuum of sexuality is based on binary opposition:
heterosexuality and homosexuality at opposite ends. Bisexuality falls
in the middle as an incompletion, a mixture, a split or two parts or

halves rather than a whole. Bisexuality itself is fluid, meaning different things to different people identified as or identifying as bisexual. Rust (1992) presents the theory of sexuality as a "trichotomy" with bisexuality being qualitatively different from hetero and homosexualities.

Bisexuality rejects the norm/deviance model. In doing so, bisexuals become politically suspect, or are seen as political cowards. They are defined as illegitimate and politically regressive, and many who face this conflict succumb and pledge allegiance to one of the politically legitimate categories, whether it be the dominant hetero or subordinate homo. The "concept of immutable sexual identity' is a political strategy used by both the dominant and marginal discourses. "Bisexuals by their very existence sabotage that strategy" (Shuster, 1987:66).

> Our disbelief in bisexuality works to women's advantage
> ... [because it] ensures their inclusion in the lesbian subculture ... (Murphy, 1990:88)

Biphobia, as exemplified in the above quotation, is one of the ways an oppressed group has become oppressive, or acts out internalised prejudices from the oppressors.

> If we only replicate the system that has oppressed us, then are we as progressive as we would like to think we are?
> ... When a system that oppresses us now has us fighting over which ones of us are 'truly' queer, we must begin to ask ourselves why we are fighting each other and not the system (Blasingame, 1992:49-50; see also Orlando, 1991).

Queer Politics is opposed to the assimilationist and conformist elements of lesbian and gay politics by acknowledging the diversity within the homosexual group: "straight queers, bi-queers, tranny queers, lez queers, fag queers, SM queers ..." (Queer Politics Now Leaflet London, 1991). Hence, queer is welcomed as breaking up lesbian and gay orthodoxes and making possible new alliances across gender and other disparate identities. However, some writers who have welcomed queer politics are also wary of the "danger of denying our heterogeneity in favour of a false 'queer nationalism'. Can the new radical grouping of 'queer nation' lead in the direction of an equally narrow and homogenising politics where specific differences are ignored?" (Smyth, 1992:28; see also Elliott, 1992). Bennett provides an example of this when she warns of the tendency by some bisexuals to declare, "everyone is really bisexual" (1992:228).

Some queer activists accuse gays and lesbians of being heterosexist, of complicity with the patriarchal heterosexual world and simply replicating its privileges and hierarchies, particularly in terms of class and race.

> Like growing up and discovering how much we resemble our parents, lesbian and gay communities are finding out how much we resemble heterosexist society (Gibian, 1992:11).

## 8.3 Feminism and Responsible Non-monogamy

Monogamy, particularly in relation to marriage, has been a significant issue for political debate and contestation for feminists. They often draw upon the writings of economic theorists such as Frederick Engels who saw monogamous marriage as transforming the nuclear family into the basic economic unit of society. Within this unit, a woman and her children became dependent upon and therefore oppressed by an individual man as representative of the state. Another influential source is Wilhelm Reich who defined a "sex-economic morality" that eliminates the subjugation described by Engels and challenges the patriarchal double standard, (based upon the myth of women's monogamous "nature" and man's nonmonogamous "nature"), and the concern over women's fidelity in order to guarantee patrilineage.

For example, Lewis sees the need for feminism to problematise coerced monogamy as the "institutionalisation of male domination and hierarchies of sexual power between individuals (men and women) in our society" (1982:88). Yet feminist problematisation of monogamy needs to occur in the context of certain "qualifications": how women have been and can be exploited through nonmonogamy particularly if the "sexual revolution" of the sixties and seventies has made women feel coerced to engage in multisexual relationships that are also oppressive; how women are ill-prepared, as gendered subjects raised in this society, to deal with the potential losses – personally, socially, economically – in becoming nonmonogamous, and the difficulty imagining alternatives due to the lack of role models, mentors and affirmation to explore; the need to consider that the economic and socio-cultural contexts of the lives of many women "necessitates monogamy as their/our only option for survival" and may indeed provide some protection for women. Hence, political questions need to be asked "not in order to articulate some polemical indictment of monogamous practice" but to examine these coercions, such as economic, structural, cultural, that "normalise" a specific sexual choice and render alternatives as "deviant". Part of this examination should include reproduction and mothering in the light of nonmonogamous alternatives.

Thus, in her work, Lewis is very aware of avoiding a binary argument that may become oppressive in endeavouring to eliminate oppression, that is, constructing a new nonmonogamous norm that creates new sets of coercions and does not assist women in shifting and challenging the realities of their specific economic, social and cultural life-contexts. Thus, she believes the work for feminists in this area is urgent but it needs to be undertaken as part of the overall resistance to patriarchal institutionalised constructs of power and property and in ways that do not "produce conservative notions of monolith, but which enable an understanding of ongoing struggle, of dealing with contradictions, and of process, not repressing" (1982: 89-99).

Smyth (1992) also believes feminism is often trapped in perceptions and constructions of binaries in its political challenges. As Adams questions

> If you can't be sure that the other Xs, Ys or Zs are going to be sympathetic to your additional identity as a V or W, with whom will you organise? (1989:28).

Jacklin writes, "Because heterosexuality has been an established sexual preference, 'I am heterosexual' also says, 'I am traditional'. At the very least it connotes that I do not have to struggle with society". Women who live nonmonogamous heterosexual lives, particularly if married or in long-term multipartnerships as the so-called "other woman", often do find themselves sited as socio-cultural outsiders (1993:34). The "heterosexual cushion can be an illusion" for these women (Crawford, 1993:44). Heterosexual feminists in long-term relationships such as Rowland (1993) contest the universalism of statements like the following:

> To be heterosexual, all a woman needs to do is to fall unthinkingly in with what everyone else does. She does not have to make a choice between equally valid alternatives ... she merely has to follow the dominant mores (Thompson, 1993:170).

According to Geller (1983), the issue of monogamy has become a significant one for lesbian-feminists. Possessiveness and jealousy are viewed as "politically incorrect", a "vestige of our patriarchal heritage cast-off along with panty-hose, bras and other artifacts" (1983:44). The dilemma with this is the fact that it could become coercive and she advocates the need for "care and patience" with each other as lesbians make their choices about "whom to love and how to love" (45).

Feminists such as Sonia Johnson have attempted to transcend or move beyond the binarily constructed monogamy/nonmonogamy debate. She calls this debate a "classic thought-loop":

> for at least the last quarter century the argument over which is more patriarchal has raged in the women's movement ...if, being as brilliant as we are, in twenty-five years we haven't been able to make any headway ...it has been the wrong debate to be having all along ...something phallocracy has deliberately distracted us from noticing (1990:110–111).

Johnson states that the "dichotomousness" of the debate is one of the "prized tools of mind control" to prevent women from exploring other ways of connecting with people (1990:112). The necessary questions for feminists are:

> What are the links between and among freedom, power, creativity, intimacy and integrity that bind them so closely that we can't have one without the others? Do we mate only in captivity? What would love look like in freedom? (112–113).

The monogamy/nonmonogamy debate becomes irrelevant. Jealousy exists only in the context of this debate so it also becomes a "nonconcept" as it is unimaginable without the concept of ownership, competition and feelings of self-inadequacy. The debate and concepts of jealousy are still man-made discourses. Feminists need to transcend this by developing "non-coercive, non-exploitative" modes of relationships beyond sexual ownership and "sleeping around" or objectifying people, both being what she calls "male style" (116).

Unfortunately, Johnson's ability to transcend either/or structures and debates does not extend to marriage/relationship. One is either in a sexually exclusive couple relationship or one isn't:

> Whatever they may think, they have committed themselves, have in a very real, very clear way, promised fidelity – regardless of what they may think or if any pronouncement they may have made to the contrary – simply by acceding to the form. To follow the form is to agree to and to make the promise. (1990: 116–117).

It is difficult to connect Johnson's thinking about non-coercion, non-dichotomy and the need to challenge phallocratic relationship structures and dream of "a love that encompasses everything and possesses nothing" to her flat denial of people's choices in redefining marital/relationship structures (118). As the examples from Australia later in this paper illustrate, feminist principles are a significant factor in negotiating successful sexual, domestic, career, child-rearing and other realities within multipartnerships.

## 8.4 Marital Nonmonogamy and Multiple Relationships

> [Traditional Patriarchal] Marriage: A community consisting of a master, a mistress, and two slaves, making in all, two (Ambrose Bierce, in Geller, 1990:104).

Social policies inscribe the heterosexual married unit as the heart of the organisation of the social field, and there are punishments and restrictions for those who do not conform. Nevertheless, historical, cross-cultural and contemporary research continues to reveal the diversity of marital relationships: couples do not always live together, are not always in "romantic" love, may have primary partners who are not their spouses, and may not be heterosexual (Whitney, 1990; Buxton, 1991; George, 1993). Hence, sexual and marital identity is not a private, individual or partnership matter of personal choice. It is constrained and defined by cultural, social and political generalities.

Anapol writes of the need for a "middle ground between the free love/do your own thing doctrine of the Sexual Revolution and outmoded lifelong monogamy" (1992:ix). The "conflict" or "clash" between individuals' nonmonogamous needs and desires, and the socially constructed and largely dysfunctional monogamous tradition, must be seen as a legitimate reason to develop new forms of relationships which synthesise elements of and transcend traditional marital alternatives. Multipartner relationships is seen as this alternative. It combines traditional concepts of commitment, love and "a lifelong intention to support each other in whatever ways seem appropriate" with the more controversial idea of sexually relating to more than one person at the same time with all partners fully aware of this.

### Catherine, Paul and Lucy

For fourteen years, Catherine has been what she labels, with a smile, the "illegal wife" of Paul in Adelaide, South Australia. For most of those years, Paul lived with his "legal wife" in order to coparent but saw Catherine one day on week-ends and three nights a week. This suited them fine and the arrangements were always open to negotiation. For example, Lucy had no qualms when Paul and Catherine took holidays together overseas or interstate.

About three years ago, Paul began to want his own home as he had never lived alone. He purchased a house geographically located equally distant from Lucy and Catherine. His children are able to stay with him as well as at their mother's and attend school. This has suited Lucy as she now has the freedom to pursue the varied working hours of her career and have her own time after years of chosen full-time mothering. It also suits Catherine who has never wanted to share her home with a lover and enjoys the freedom of visiting Paul. She has never wanted children and is happy that Paul would not expect her to give up her career and lifestyle to have children.

Catherine feels the relationship has worked for years because the various needs of the three seem to mesh well and all three are willing to negotiate issues and work out arrangements such as time, finances, career demands, both regularly and with flexibility. "I never thought this would last. For a few years, I kept waiting for him to do the soap opera thing on me and go back to his wife. After all, he never stopped telling me he loved her. To a certain extent, we still just live it and create it as we go along and that's exciting." She rarely sees Lucy as both women prefer this sense of separateness from each other.

The hardest parts of the relationship for Catherine have been the need for secrecy due to career, lack of understanding by family, and the undermining of her relationship by women-friends who think "a real feminist wouldn't put up with a man who thinks he can have two women in his harem. It's really hard to get them to think of the benefits in this to someone like me who does not want the fusses and tedium of a full-time live-in male lover, doesn't want children, and enjoys my own space. They think I'm being exploited. How do they know? The heterosexual women-friends seem to do a lot more accommodating and have less freedom with their supposedly faithful lovers and husbands".

*Ron and Lorissa*

When Ron and Lorissa began their "affair" at work in Melbourne, Victoria, Ron's marriage was crumbling. As months moved on, his marriage actually improved and Lorissa's marriage crumbled. "His wife found he was now less pressured, having other interests and needs fulfilled, and he could actually be with her without resenting her. So although she's not interested in getting to know me, she has no problems with the relationship and indeed jokes that "the other woman has made him a better husband"".

Unfortunately, Lorissa's husband at first thought he could handle the situation, and seemed to derive "some sort of pleasure in another man lusting after his wife. But that's the problem, see. I was still his property. He was lending me out like a really valuable piece of jewellery that someone else can wear but have to return to whom it really belongs. When he began to wake up and notice this was more than lust and I actually was not owned by him, he felt threatened and all his patriarchal insecurities flooded him. Since then, he's moved out of home, leaving me with the children as some sort of punishment, is having casual flings with young women and it bothers him that what bothers me is not what he's doing but whether he's exploiting the young women. And it bothers him that when he threatens to divorce me, I don't beg him to come back. So while my relationship with my husband has been exposed for the patriarchal shallowness it really was, and I am glad that's happened, Ron's relationship with his wife has revealed itself to be a really great thing once the pressures to conform were off and Ron could develop other parts of his life. Oh well, that's the way things go. The hardest part is external judgement. I'll never forget the night Ron had a bad heart attack and the doctors and nurses at the hospital just could not cope with both his wife and me worrying over him, kissing him and declaring that we were both entitled to knowledge about his health, operation, medication. They really wanted me to feel cheap and his wife to feel like a demented idiot for allowing this."

### Rick, Mandy and Andrew

Mandy's two male partners live in different cities, Adelaide South Australia and Melbourne, Victoria. Andrew is bisexual. She travels to them as her work is far more flexible and she has grown equally fond of both cities and the lifestyles and networks they provide. She feels very lucky as she has had the opportunity to live two parallel lives for the last five years with two men, one a husband of fourteen years and the other her "husband" of five years. Both bring out certain qualities in her as well as respect her independence and support her work. They rarely see each other and only communicate over the telephone in order to relay messages to Mandy. Negotiation, co-operation and trust that she loves them both make the relationships work. The benefits the men gain is freedom from the traditional rules full-time wives might impose on men. Both are very independent men who have strong feminist principles. "Both choose to be monogamous with me but it's up to them." Her husband equally cares for the school-age children. The geographical separateness of the relationships assists as the relationships are complete entities in themselves in different cities with different sets of work demands and friendship circles. "I can switch off one part of me and tune into another, so I tend to always feel fresh and energised, and look forward to seeing them". The most difficult time was establishing the relationship. "We had no-one who lived like us to talk to. No role models. We hurt each other, we hurt other people we loved, and did some horrific things. But somehow we made it." The most difficult issues are the need to remain closeted, the amount of editing and lying that occurs with family and some friends in order not to create hurt and misunderstanding in others, and the lack of socio-cultural and legal recognition of her relationship with Andrew. "It's not a de facto. It's not a marriage. There's no public word for it." Frustrations include knowing that some people, especially other men, would think her husband was weak "rather than recognising how strong he is and how much I love him", the way her bisexual partner is scorned by some gay men, and the way some gay men tend to think she does not know of his bisexuality "and so they construct this picture of the poor little woman who has no idea". "It's also a problem for some feminists who think relating to one man is bad enough, what woman would want two? It's also been interesting discovering what I call the armchair feminists. Like the academic who said, "How can your husband allow this?" That question certainly shocked me coming from a self-defined radical feminist."

Mandy would readily go back to monogamy should one of the relationships fail in the future. "I was very happy in a monogamous relationship for nine years. I then met Andrew and I knew my marriage would suffer if I didn't pursue my happiness with him as well. Now, they're two wonderful relationships with the inevitable tough times and questioning long-term relationships experience. I discovered for myself how stereotypical and silly all this hype about "the affair" really is. I'm not having an "affair". I'm in two ordinary great relationships, if you know what I mean by that supposed contradiction. I also know that should I ever need to I can live by myself surrounded by wonderful, loving friends."

The above forms of nonmonogamy are open to attack from the dominant discourse of lifelong monogamous marital relationships as well as from those who oppose the construct of marriage itself. Young (1993), for example, calls for the abolition of marriage because "it draws a line between legitimate and illegitimate relationships", is the "cornerstone of patriarchal power" and a "significant regulator of social norms" such as in its privileging of heterosexual couples. Thus "the institution of marriage is irreparably unjust". Young does not seem to consider that marriage forms can be diversified and indeed seen as options in relationship structures alongside other equally viable relationship structures. In other words, the problem may lie not in marriage itself but the political, economic and social meanings imbued into what should be a form of private relationship between two or more people. Elizabeth Grosz, a significant Australian feminist, delivered very insightful lectures, based on a working paper, in 1993 about the need for expansion, freedom, movement, and pleasure in our sexual and interpersonal lives. She not only dismissed bisexuality because "the indeterminacy is worrying" and "bisexuals are in a luxurious position of wanting to eat their cake and have it too without having to pay for this luxury" but labelled traditional heterosexual relationships as "boring and stale" while nontraditional nonmonogamous heterosexual relationships were scoffed at as "naive 1960s polysexualism".

> Everyone from feminist scholars to men's magazines has enshrined monogamous commitment ... as if there were no sensible middle ground between marriage and bacchanalia ... As if it were humanly impossible to be devoted to two [or more] lovers (Talbot, 1992:68).

The above example illustrates the awareness of moving beyond the binary oppositions. Talbot asks: "Why not strive for a sexual pluralism that offers men and women more than one formula for intimacy?" (1992:74). A variety of relationship niches allows everyone to find a place which fits their individual needs and desires. Thus, as Turney (1993), spokesperson for the Beyond Monogamy Inc movement in Australia states, nonmonogamy is not for everyone and it would not be upheld as the new superior lifestyle form.

Yoshizaki, a married bisexual feminist of mixed Japanese-American background, also writes of heterosexual marriages or relationships having "a history of rigid rules that plague them" (1992:156). Her multiplicity of marginalities – ethnicity, gender, sexuality and nonmonogamous marriage – leads to conflicts with established discourses and community mores but also diverse vantage points from which to define her own parameters, synthesising and transcending the established constructs through her multiple intersecting.

### Soulla and Keith

Soulla migrated from Greece with her family in her early teens. She met Keith while working in a factory in Sydney. From the beginning she loved him because "he was not rough and never laughed at my poor English, my funny clothes, the way I knew nothing about sex and was so shy" and seemed to respect the expectations her family had of her as a young woman. Thus, he agreed to chaperoned outings, a quick wedding conducted Greek style, and allowing his two daughters to be raised in the Greek Orthodox Church. After a few years of marriage, he became depressed for months and then finally admitted that although he loved Soulla, Keith could no longer hide from her or from himself the fact that he was gay. He had fallen in love with a man he wanted to see regularly but he would be devastated if Soulla left him or took the children away from him.

Soulla recalls the next few years being those of great anger and frustration where each at different points tried to commit suicide. Her religious background and being part of a strict Greek community prevented her from ending the marriage because of the shame it would bring to her family. Keith's feelings of being trapped and having caused so much pain to the woman he loved was more than he could bear. With time, they found the pain began to ease. There was too much love between them and equal parenting of their daughters, as well as the shared hard work to get above their working-class backgrounds, to get divorced and face the psychological, emotional and economic traumas.

They still live together, their daughters are adolescents and thrive with their father's understanding and parenting. They both know he is gay. There is very little sex between Keith and Soulla and at first Soulla found it difficult to accept "Keith made love to me because he loved me emotionally but he wasn't really lusting after me. But then, that early lust stuff seems to die in most marriages anyway. At least, I've always had the physical affection, kisses, cuddles, a great sensitive person to talk to." Indeed, Soulla feels that compared to the many married men she knows and hears about, there is no way she would give him up. "He is a wonderful husband and father and my best friend. Other women envy me because he is just so caring. And if they knew the truth, they'd spit at him. It's so stupid. But I would have done the same once." Her religious faith has also sustained her in "knowing there is a reason for everything". She is now very ill and cannot leave her bed after battling cancer for two years "and I know why God sent him to me. The love, devotion and care he has given me is the answer. Knowing that when I die, the girls are in good hands." Keith has a male lover of four years who is supporting him emotionally as he cares for his wife.

*Maria and Bill*

Bill married Maria in Adelaide, a second-generation Italian woman, hoping that his feelings of homosexuality would subside. They didn't. Ten years and two children later, he came out to her. They separated but somehow could not bring themselves to divorce. There was always something that drew them together, especially her Italian extended family and community. Although they knew of his homosexuality, he found her parents and most other members of her community wanted him to be present at festivals, weddings and other parties. "They loved me for who I was, and the way I was a good father to my children. That surprised me. I thought they'd be so homophobic. You know, the stereotype of Italian migrants and other ethnics as homophobic. So we've remained married, and are the best of friends. Our kids are young adults now and Maria has fallen in love with an Italian man but she still loves me. I'm encouraging her to develop this relationship, the fact a man is just sexually so interested in her is good for her. I'm reassuring her I'll always be there for her whatever happens with him. He's a bit homophobic and jealous of me. He's confused about us but he's a good man in other ways. I think they may want to live together soon. Yes, I've had two strong relationships with other men in those years. I never was one for casual sex anyway, I don't have a lover at the moment. Anyway, I'm helping to care for a toddler grandson and by the end of the day, I'm exhausted."

Buxton (1991) found that many heterosexual spouses do not necessarily want a marriage to end if a partner is gay, lesbian or bisexual. There may be a strong bond that both partners do not wish to break and they come to see themselves as life partners and redefine the meaning of marriage to suit themselves. Partners in gay-straight relationships must deal with the issue that the outside world, whether it be heterosexual or homosexual worlds, will rarely consider the relationship valid. As one of Buxton's interviewees stated,

> Our relationship has internal validity regardless of outside standards ... It took a while for us to write this script for ourselves. We've survived seven years of marriage by tolerating the ambivalence of what we are and what could happen (1991:231-234).

This is an example of transcending the codes of both mainstream (in terms of marriage) and the marginal (in terms of sexuality). Buxton concludes that a "comprehensive view of the polarised gay-straight controversy is sorely needed" and the solutions will be found "between the extreme positions" of traditional monogamous exclusively heterosexual marriage and exclusively homosexual partnerships. Alternative marriage and family arrangements need to be explored (1991:275; see also Nahas and Turley, 1979; Gochros, 1989).

As one couple related to Catherine Whitney in her study of gay men and straight women,

> We are a gay man and a heterosexual woman who have enjoyed a monogamous union for three years. Our experience has been a real surprise, a source of confusion and consternation. We perceive life to have a lot more gray areas than it has black and white. We wonder if categorising people and lifestyles isn't futile. We gave up our own labelling, shelved our 'what ifs', and decided to live and love, trying to accept the contradictions (1990:88).

Queer theorists argue that it is the very act of labelling and defining that limits sexuality potential as people feel they need to mould their sexuality into the available constructs. As Whitney states after interviewing gay men and heterosexual women who choose to marry and devise their own marital systems,

> marriage is sociological, not ontological. It is an institution, a design for living that requires only the commitment of two [or more] parties ... It is not necessary, for example, that a couple share the same background or the same race...same religious orientation... what about having different sexual orientations? (1990: 82).

If in other parts of our lives, we do not strive to be static beings, but value growth, development and change, why should our sexual beings and marital relationships be any different? This notion of sexual and marital stasis says, "you must stay still so we can see who you are" (Gibian, 1992:3). Anapol (1992) believes nonmonogamists could be the last sexual minority to come out of hiding. She believes monogamy and promiscuity are also on a continuum rather than being a dichotomy as most people are somewhere inbetween. Very few people have one lifelong relationship and very few have never had an exclusive relationship for at least a brief period of time. She also sees "responsible nonmonogamists" as making and/both choices in an either/or world.

> Monogamy for me had been an uncomfortable either/or balancing act- freedom or intimacy, flexibility or loyalty, change or commitment. Polygamy [provided] ... Stability and excitement. Security and freedom. Intimacy and inclusiveness. Depth and diversity (1992:111).

She believes a relationship can be both personal and nonexclusive, focussed on several partners in a multifocus and multilevel association. Assimilating to the monogamous mainstream may be due to "frustration rather than conviction". Others who choose the nonmonogamous marginality find their lifestyles closeted due to fear of socio-economic and familial repercussions (1992:84). By choosing a multiple partner relationship, Anapol believes an individual is placing oneself "in the center of the cyclone" confronting "opposing forces" from the powerful monogamous heterosexual marital mainstream (which in reality involves a majority of husbands and wives having secret extramarital relationships) and the power-challenging nonmonogamous, nonmarital marginality (which in reality usually involves serial monogamy or a series of monogamous relationships). Nearing speaks in terms of a synthesis model, albeit hierarchical, when she writes that multiple partnerships are really "taking the best of the old ways and evolving something new and improved" (1992:82).

## 8.5 Responsible Nonmonogamy in Australia

Australian women's magazines are still presenting remedies and howtos to sustain monogamous relationships, or presenting serial monogamy as the "nineties way of loving", or rarely touching upon multipartnerships and only as grim warnings of the inevitable disaster. Hence, the either/or binary has not been transcended. For example NEW WOMAN (January, 1994), which is intended to cater for feminist-minded independent women, presented "serial monogamy" as the "alternative way of loving and living" where a past relationship must be given up in order to move onto a new and vastly improved one, and of course, that one will also be surrendered once a better one is found. The multipartner choice is not provided although the writer, Angela Neustatter, interviews a psychologist, a sociologist and a lecturer in nursing who state that serial monogamy suits outgoing confident people who can cope with rejection and can deal with the turmoil of breaking up and starting again only to find that similar problems are met a few years later in the next relationship. This article provided no analysis of the myths and cultural assumptions that construct people's expectations of a relationship or meanings prescribed to words such as "romance" "love", and how relationships evolve. Nor does it question why people must surrender a relationship that may have many important qualities in order to begin a new one which will also have important qualities and reveal its flaws years later. Nor does it analyse the effects of divorces and familial disruption on some children.

Articles like Elisabeth Winkler's in COSMOPOLITAN do acknowledge that there can be more than one "Mr Right" and then proceeds to illustrate the "hell", "conflict", "double trouble" that is the only result of multipartner relationships.

Sporadic appearances of people on television who discuss their nonmonogamous lifestyles do occur such as Sue Metzenrath, a nonmonogamous bisexual woman currently in three ongoing relationships, who discussed her life in positive terms based on feminist analysis (DR FEELGOOD, 27th August, 1994). However, one member of the audience, a married monogamous woman, pointed out that Sue's discussion was offensive not in the lifestyle she was presenting, which the audience-member believed was her valid choice, but in the explicitly pronounced assumption that women who were in monogamous marriages were automatically repressed. The audience-member was pointing out the potential oppressiveness of people such as Ms Metzenrath challenging traditional lifestyles only to construct new forms of conformity, hence merely reversing binarily-constructed hierarchies.

Stephen A. Davis (1991) has written a book in conjunction with channeller Lyssa Royal which is readily available in Australia. It examines the religious, legal, media and personal premises that underlie the enforcement of monogamy as "normal" and/or "natural". He concludes that monogamy "is dead" considering the amount of marriages involved in one way or another with nonmonogamy in its open or secretive forms. He examines the part played by fear in not disrupting the "monogamy myth" and how this myth needs to be disrupted before monogamy as a valid choice can be established. Davis presents the story of how his own marital relationship evolved, both easily and painfully, to a responsible nonmonogamous situation, polyfidelity, which is a commitment to more than one person at the same time.

As Davis points out, fear and lack of support and role modelling prevent people from choosing to live a responsible nonmonogamous lifestyle. Supportive networks for "ethical nonmonogamists" are springing up in Australia such as the previously mentioned Beyond Monogamy. Turney (1993) states this movement is at an historical point in time where gay liberationists, feminists, multiculturalists, Aboriginal activists have all previously been: at the beginning of a long road to social justice via public awareness, understanding, acceptance, and recognition in socio-political structures.

> There are no equal opportunity laws enforcing the rights of ethical nonmonogamists, and the current level of public misunderstanding calls for a major public information

campaign (1993:27).

Turney's television and other personal appearances, newsletter publication, and making available pamphlets and other resource material and names of contact persons and contact groups around Australia, particularly in 1992-1993, has led to the creation of small but growing networks in most Australian states. Originating in Perth, Western Australia, Beyond Monogamy Inc is one of the world's 12 non-profit educational support associations for those involved in "honest, balanced, intimate relationships of three or more adults". It offers regular social meetings, a lending library, referral to qualified marriage counsellors, doctors and lawyers, a speakers bureau and personal consultations. By early 1993, Beyond Monogamy Inc had a mailing list of more than 70 singles, couples, threesomes, and foursomes either interested or involved in nonmonogamy. The single most common group in Australia, according to people who are part of the mailing list or openly discuss their lives with Turney, is a threesome with one woman and two men followed closely by a foursome of two couples. Mostly due to social pressure, such groups rarely live in the same house. Turney acknowledges that multipartnering is "definitely not a lifestyle suitable for most" due to internalised socio-cultural constructions and/or personal choice and he knows the "trial by fire" responsible nonmonogamists often undergo in terms of personal upheavals, societal discriminations and condemnations:

> We ask not that all of you try to become polygamous but that all of you at least respect our freedom, and not speak ill of us unless you fully understand our motivations, experiences, and unique etiquettes (1993:27).

Turney believes "the future looks good for polyfidelity" as "an enlightened world comes to accept the beauty and diversity of each of its citizens" and thus there will be more public acknowledgement of these lifestyles in Australia.

A more recent example comes from Jackie Huggins, the most published Aboriginal feminist writer/activist in Australia:

> I fell in love with, horror of horrors, a married man who was all I ever hoped to meet in my life ... his wife and half the Murries [term for Aboriginal people] in Australia knew who he was. The full emotional intensity of my love for Reg [pseudonym] lasted for thirteen years. To this day I remain firm friends with him, his wife Margie [pseudonym] and family. In fact Margie and I became close allies. Polygamy rules and I will always be known as "his other wife" (1994: 332).

In conversation with Jackie Huggins, she told me it was about time she acknowledged this part of her history and its significance in terms of how Aboriginal peoples had differing notions of relationships and sexuality that have been disrupted and viewed negatively by Western, Judaeo-Christian colonisers (see also Gays and Lesbians Aboriginal Alliance, 1994). Other feminists are also examining the impact of colonial values and economic systems on pre-colonial relationship structures and disrupting eurocentric and androcentric anthropological interpretations of such models, such as the work of Ralston (1988) with polyandry, or women with more than one husband, in Polynesian communities.

Some members of the growing men's movement in Australia are also beginning to challenge both monogamy and "irresponsible non-monogamy" as patriarchal constructs. Men's movement activists such as David Dendy (1994) draw from feminist theory in recognising monogamy as serving "to enslave women as sexual property". From a psychological perspective, and unfortunately veering toward universalist judgements, he writes:

> monogamy isolates and encourages overly dependent relationships, within which the most horrific violence and abuse are often hidden. On an interpersonal level, monogamy seems to be held together through jealousy, possessiveness and fear rather than any noble values (1994:16).

Dendy explains that men challenging monogamy as the only valid relationship model in our society are not returning to "a sexual permissiveness based on traditional masculine sexual values of objectification" as occurred in the name of women's sexual liberation in the sixties but writes that "it feels oppressive of me to pressure my partner to put limits on her relationships" and acknowledges that this "journey" beyond men's rights over women's sexuality "both scares and excites me":

> I too am attached to the idea of possessing my loved one, and to the idea that I ought to be the only one (1994: 16).

## 8.6 Conclusion: The Closets are Opening

> She declined to be pigeon-holed, dissected and neatly compartmentalised. She would be what she wanted when she wanted ... She put on all her hats at once (Choe, 1992:24).

This article aimed to demonstrate the limitations, oppressions, and silencing of realities inherent in the need to homogenise, categorise and simplify as conducted by both mainstream powerful groups and marginal power-challenging groups when discussing responsible non-monogamy and traditional monogamy. In so doing, a multiplicity of places is upheld which recognises what can be termed, "multiplaced persons". As Bernard writes, "Not only does marriage have a future, it has many futures" and traditional monogamous relationships will be one of the options made available in a world that openly acknowledges "the enormous difference among human beings ... it will come to seem incongruous that everyone has to be forced into an identical mold" (1982: 270-271). Bernard adds that with options will come other demands and no form of relationship "guarantees utopia". Nevertheless, choosing not to choose monogamy allows for choices that better suit individuals at specific points in time.

Ethnic, sexual, gender and marital identifications are about flux and fixing. Identities are "precarious unities of conflicting desires and social commitments" (Weeks, 1987:49). Silvana, a participant in my past research, deals with this dichotomy of flux and fixing on an individual level in the following words:

> I don't want to be boxed in. Defining myself in any way is a problem ... [and] whenever I speak I am constantly making myself. (Pallotta-Chiarolli, 1992).

"Multiplaced" persons may find weaving through a complex web of social relations far easier than "placed persons" who can only deal with difference from a narrow categorical position that defines everything outside itself as the inferior "other". The "complex web" has intricate patterns and points of contact that afford a greater interconnectedness between all its inhabitants, such that in acknowledging diversity in others and in oneself, new unities may be forged.

Past socio-cultural ideological conclusions and solutions need to be deconstructed to reveal the negations and omissions that made them temporarily possible. Asian-Australian lesbian Happy Ho presents the following powerful metaphorical declaration:

> This is a time of unrest. The world is losing its boundaries. The Wall has fallen and the closets are opening ... [As] displaced persons We live with a code of our own (De Ishtar and Sitka, 1991:8).

The "boundaries" of social ascription appear to be loosening while the "closets" in which persons hide due to negative community acknowledgement are opening. Thus, the realities of lived experiences can be acknowledged and exploitative and discriminatory realities and ideologies be challenged. And an important factor encouraging these shifts is personal agency, the running "against the grain" in pursuit of a personal identity and relationship model negotiated from constantly shifting options.

# Acknowledgements

My gratitude and appreciation to the people who have openly discussed their nonmonogamous lifestyles with me over the years and recently.

Theoretical components of this paper were published in 1995 in the book *Voices of a Margin: Speaking For Yourself*, edited by J. McNamee and L. Rowan, Rockhampton, University of Central Queensland Press.

# Chapter 9

# The History of Non-monogamous Lifestyles: A Historical and Cross-cultural Survey

K. Lano

## 9.1 Introduction

This article will survey the forms of non-monogamy that exist in present societies and that have occurred in past societies. In particular we will try and answer the question "under what circumstances is non-monogamy a liberated or progressive aspect of society", and we will examine the links between the forms of non-monogamy present in a society and other aspects of that society (for example, its attitude to sexuality or to women).

## 9.2 The Suppression of Non-monogamy

The meaning and nature of relationships has varied widely across different cultures over the last 5000 years. The Western model of exclusive monogamy between a man and woman of the same generation has been far from a universal norm, with some cultures, such as the Polynesian, having no institution of 'marriage' or words for 'husband' or 'wife', and accepting polyamorous lifestyles for men and women (Diamond, 1992). Even in Western cultures there has been considerable variation in family structure, with a number of subcultures and religious communities (of which the largest was probably the Mormon state of Utah in the USA) supporting non-monogamous lifestyles.

Non-monogamy in relationships, despite its prevalence (10% of men in the US Janus survey had participated in 'open marriage', 14% in threesomes; Reibstein reports that over 50% of married men have affairs), is still among the most stigmatised of behaviours (in the recent Wellcome survey in the UK (Wellings, 1994), over 80% of men and women believed sex outside marriage was wrong). Conflict over monogamy versus non-monogamy was one of the main reasons why lesbian couples broke up in the survey of (Becker, 1988). The idea that sexual relationships must be exclusive is now a core aspect of Western social beliefs, and the possibility of being in more than one significant relationship concurrently is discounted. In the past, 'adultery' was punished by death, as indeed it still is in some countries (such as Iran) today. Capitalism and Western religions have emphasised monogamy as a means of controlling and confining sexuality within a strictly reproductive role and, formally, as a means of establishing clear (property-owning) male lines of descent. Asian cultures, particularly the Chinese, have also instituted grotesque punishments, mainly on women, for adultery (Diamond, 1992).

Laws have made non-monogamy illegal and valid grounds for divorce. In the USA, the Mormons were persecuted for decades until they renounced (a patriarchal form of) polygamy as an element of their religion. Many laws based on the assumptions of conventional monogamous marriage are still in force, in only slightly modified forms, which mean that people who wish to create alternative forms of relationship must draw up explicit contracts to define the details of ownership and inheritance (Hodgekinson, 1988).

In contrast, non-capitalist societies such as Iron-age Britain, Polynesian and Nepalese cultures, have adopted polygamous or polyandrous ways of organising relationships. In the polyandrous cultures of Iron-age Europe, it has been suggested that this was linked with architecture, with circular building styles being preferred over rectilinear styles (Ehrenberg, 1989).

The idea that one close affectional relationship should exclude all others is culturally specific, and with several other concepts of relationships, is quite recent. In previous centuries, and presently in some Asian cultures, 'love' has been regarded as akin to insanity, and has been discouraged because it disrupted social stability and distracted effort from economic imperatives. In the (relatively) less repressed societies of the modern West there should in theory be more acceptance of variety in relationship structures, and a greater concern for personal development and fulfilment as an aim of relationships, rather than economic or lineage concerns. These beliefs also mean that non-monogamy could be progressive and liberated.

In the West, experiments in non-monogamous living have occurred in alternative religious and political communities, most significantly in the communes of the 60s counter-culture. The 'poly' community in the US is a descendent of the commune movement, and organises an annual conference, support groups and literature. Also in the US are the 'safe sex' or 'jack and jill off' parties in California and the East Coast. These are orgies which are conducted according to strict safe sex and consent guidelines, and are a means of challenging the sex-negative messages which have dominated the AIDS era.

## 9.3 Non-monogamy in Historical Perspective

Some authors, such as (Hite, 1994), argue that there has been a consistent 3000 year history of the 'patriarchal' monogamous family, which replaced more diverse forms in which women had a higher status. In this view, monogamy was enforced so that a clearly defined male lineage could be identified, through which authority descended from generation to generation. The original concept of the family was simply the mother/child group, and Hite sees the current rise of single parent families as a guide to the future form of family structures.

In contrast to this view, it seems that historically quite diverse family structures have existed, with monogamy being enforced more strictly in societies with a centralised or hierarchical power structure. In the case of Polynesian society, the gradual transformation of this society from an 'authority free' structure in which positions of power of one individual over a group did not exist, into one with an entrenched hierarchy of leaders, seemed to correlate with an increase in the rigidity of relationship forms. Similarly, highly authoritarian states such as Victorian England had the most constrained concepts of sexual behaviour. Thus non-monogamy might not be suppressed just for patriarchal reasons, but because diversity in family structures made government in general more difficult (individual acceptance of arbitrary authority was reduced), and positions of authority less clearly marked out.

This is not to argue that non-monogamy is automatically associated with progressive trends in a society. In societies such as the Mormons or modern-day Islamic societies, in which women have a low status, the way non-monogamy is practised simply reflects this low status and is organised around the needs of high status men. In addition, an expectation to adhere to non-monogamy, as in some lesbian communities (Becker, 1988) can be nearly as oppressive and harmful as an expectation to adhere to monogamy.

A general human priority has also been that the upbringing of children is carried out in a reliable manner. This has been seen as a justification for strict monogamy. However this is not necessarily the case in all societies – in the traditional Hebrew society described in the Bible for example there are instances of a man marrying his brothers wife on the death of the brother, in order to perpetuate this family. In addition, it is clear that reproduction and the perpetuation of a 'clan' are more important in the Old Testament than the details of the relationships between the people who are doing this reproduction (eg, incest is an acceptable means of perpetuating a lineage in the case of Lot and his daughters, and female servants an acceptable substitute for 'barren' wives). The examples of Polynesian society, and of the communes in the modern West, shows that the upbringing of children can be reliably and successfully performed without conventional marital structures.

Hostility to alternative ways of sexual relating (and in particular to "pretended families" or alternative ways of organising childcare and upbringing) has been a constant of Western capitalist society, from the attacks on the Mormons to the Labouchère amendment of 1885 (which aimed to outlaw *any* homosexual behaviour, and homosexual lifestyles, rather than just buggery, which had previously been the case), Clause 28 in 1987, and the virulent attacks on gay adoption and lesbian mothers up to the present. The ideology of the patriarchal monogamous family became dominant in the late 19th century and all proposed alternatives were seen as threats to the very nature of society and strongly resisted.

Attitudes to sexuality and sexual relations have not necessarily been revised as a result of increasing political awareness in other areas. For a long time European communist and Trotskyist parties defended the (post Stalin) Soviet oppression of homosexuals and discouraged homosexuals from becoming members because they were regarded as a security risk. The classic Marxist view of sex was as a single 'natural' biological force which had been distorted under capitalism, but which would be liberated in a socialist state:

> "Monogamy, instead of collapsing, [will] at last become a reality" (Weeks, 1990: 145)

Their view of what this 'natural' sexuality consisted of was thus only a slight variation on the Christian conventions of relationships.

Anarchist and libertarian socialist theories and movements have consistently been the most advanced in their views, from the (at the time) radical writings of Carpenter to the experiments with group living that took place in the sixties counter-culture.

### 9.3.1 Ancient Greece

Monogamy was the norm in the city states of ancient Greece, although the practice of men having concubines was widespread (in Athens a man could found several legitimate but separate families via concubines). The coexistence of homosexual teacher/student relationships between an older and younger man, and conventional marriage, was also a consistent aspect of Greek society. Divorce was relatively easy, although women in general had low status relative to men.

### 9.3.2 Egypt

Detailed records of ancient Egyptian society only exist for the New Kingdom (1570BC – 330BC). Women had a relatively high status and could participate in administration and the priesthood, however marriage was a contractual arrangement between the suitor and the woman's father. In the upper class brother/sister marriages took place, and men could construct harems, but otherwise a more conventional monogamy, sometimes with men having concubines, prevailed.

### 9.3.3 South America

A wide variety of marriage customs existed amongst the various nomadic and agricultural tribes of South America. Forest-based nomadic groups were often matrilocal and matrilineal in structure, and marriage was not regulated by religion, nor was fidelity strictly required. No special ceremonies were attached to marriage, unlike other events such as death and puberty. Chilean tribes had however a much stronger marriage custom. Few of the tropical forest tribes were entirely monogamous, with polygamy practised by men in positions of high status or power. Polyandry was practised, but rarely.

### 9.3.4 South Asia

The Himalayan tribes had a considerable tolerance for premarital or extramarital sex, although clan exogamy (marriage and relationships outside the clan) was enforced. The caste system and caste endogamy has also been a pervasive feature of South Asian cultures, as has the dowry system. Polyandry was practised by the Sherpa, Bhotia and Lepcha groups. These relationships often involved brothers and were considered to help avoid the fragmentation of family property and to increase solidarity between brothers. A similar practice, in which two or more younger brothers share an elder brother's wife, was a custom among the Tibetians, and the Khasa, Toda and Nayar. In South India today it is still possible for women to have two husbands (Diamond, 1992).

The strength of the extended family system in South Asian cultures, even when these are embedded within another culture, as in modern Europe, means that homosexual liaisons by married men are highly covert and often denied by the men concerned, who, as in North African Muslim cultures, would not see themselves as homosexual provided that they remained in an active inserter role in such liaisons (Gollain, 1995). Evidence suggests that such activities are however quite often practised.

### 9.3.5 Europe

European societies have been some of the most fanatical in their suppression of sexuality (of any kind), and of relationship diversity. The original Christians, guided by a belief that the material world was soon to disappear, tended to regard sex as, at best, a distasteful and animalistic act, and preferably one avoided altogether. Although this position moderated, the spread of Christianity over Europe in the centuries after the end of the Roman Empire set the official standards by which the morality of these societies were defined.

The concept of 'love' was very different from the meaning it came to have in the modern West. Love was supposed to be directed primarily at God, and not at other people. Even when it did occur between people, it was not connected to marriage and relationships (for example, 'courtly love' was between individuals who were not socially permitted to have relationships). Economic and status needs prevailed over individual choice, with arranged marriages being a frequent occurrence up to three generations ago (Diamond, 1992). In Victorian England a 'chaperone' system was used to monitor and constrain the liaisons between young men and women.

Some individuals did attempt to construct alternatives, such as the relationship between Sartre and Simone de Beauvoir, in which the lovers lived separately and never became a 'family' in the conventional sense. Edward Carpenter aimed to live out his own beliefs in the alternative possibilities of love and relationships, and whilst mainly monogamous, he advocated reform of marriage, with a greater stress on spiritual rather than sexual loyalty, and greater social independence for women. Carpenter presented as an ideal the 'formation of a body of friends' who would be linked by political as well as personal attachment (Weeks, 1990: 77), and did to an extent create such a group, centered on his long-time partner George Merrill.

However it was not until after the 2nd World War that major social changes and a rise in relationship diversity occurred. Even in the 50's, as (Segal, 1990) points out, the model of marriage in the UK was still of an almost business-like arrangement between the husband and wife, with little communication and with separate spheres of life being maintained.

Despite the return of more right-wing governments in Europe in the 80's and 90's, the social trends away from traditional relationship forms have continued. In the USSR 50% of marriages ended in divorce in their first year, whilst in Germany in 1993 50% of the population was unmarried. In the UK only 7% of families adhere to the traditional norm of working husband, non-working wife and children, even though this is the model held up by the government as the ideal. According to a survey by Annette Lawson in 1982, 71% of married people in the UK have some experience of extra-marital sex (74% of men and 72% of women).

## 9.3.6 Japan

Historically the attitudes to sexuality in Japan have varied significantly over time. At one stage in the early samurai society (1232) it was possible for women to inherit land, and (upper class) women had a reasonably high status compared to men. However the status and role of women became more restricted in the more authoritarian later feudal society, and families were organised as strict hierarchies with absolute obedience being demanded from family members towards the male family head, and with 'danson-johi' (respect for male, contempt for female) being promoted. Modern Japan has continued the latter tradition, with female status strongly dependent upon marriage – indeed institutions of arranged marriage and of 'trial' marriage (whereby a woman that proves to be an unsatisfactory wife can be returned, in disgrace, to her family) still continue. The geisha system provided (high-status) men with sexual freedom, but there has been only limited possibilities for liberated forms of non-monogamy or acceptance of alternative sexualities.

## 9.3.7 North America

As discussed above, the traditional Hawaiian culture did not have a marriage institution, and it was possible for one member of a couple to have a 'poly' lifestyle whilst the other was monogamous: sex outside the pair was not seen as a cause for separation. Children from partnerships were cared for by society as a whole (Mead, 1954).

Continental Indian cultures displayed a wide variety of kinship and social practices. The Great Basin Indian groups allowed sororal polygamy (the marriage of a man to two or more sisters) and fraternal polyandry (marriage of a woman to two or more brothers), although the former was typically not formalised, rather consisting of a man extending sexual access to his wife to his brother. Women had relatively high status (for example women could become shamens) and there was not a rigid social hierarchy, with leaders only being followed while they were functional for the group. In contrast the Northwest coast Indians operated a finely graded hierarchical status system in their hunter/gatherer groups, and emphasised the nuclear monogamous family. The Plains Indian culture supported a more conventional patriarchal form of polygamy, with men being able to have several wives, whilst women found guilty of infidelity could be punished by having their noses cut off. Marriages were typically arranged, with romantic love sometimes being tolerated (the Teton) or regarded as disgracing the woman (the Cheyenne). Other Indian groups, such as the Plateau Indians, gave a higher status to women, and monogamy was dominant.

The USA adopted many of the attitudes to sexuality of its originating European societies, and the suppression of the Mormons for their polygamy was only one example of how narrow the acceptable notions of sexuality were in this society (however, it was not unknown for two men to enter into a 'marriage' with the same women, in circumstances, such as the opening of the West, in which women were in extreme short supply).

The eruption of the counter-culture in the 1960s, and its associated political movements, particularly the women's and gay liberation movements, suddenly provided space in which experiments with diverse forms of relationship could take place in relative openness. The book (Rodgers, 1973) written at (what later turned out to be) the high-point of this movement, gives a survey of some of the arrangements which were practised in communes across the USA. He estimates that at this time there were 2000 - 3000 communes in the USA, generally based on an anarchist philosophy of mutual aid and independence. Forms of sexual arrangements within communes were, in order:

- pair-based, but not exclusive. In this case individuals could feel that their relationships were threatened by non-monogamy, especially if a couple came into a commune and one member was non-monogamous and the other was not;

- no sex within the group – this seemed to sometimes lead to a certain superficiality and lack of communication;

- group marriage, sometimes, as in the case of Harrad West, being organised to the extent that a chart was used to show which male/female couples were sleeping together at a particular point in time.

All of these arrangements seemed to be relatively stable. It should be realised though, that the people who lived in such communes were a small and privileged minority – Rodgers is concerned to emphasise how 'decent' and 'middle class' many of these people were. However this middle class bias itself casts doubt on how genuine much of the behaviour was – these individuals were perhaps merely acting out an ideology, and often felt in conflict with what they needed. The eventual result was disillusionment and a backlash.

Male/male sex was far less common in the communes than male/female or female/female – homophobia amongst men was still very strong at this time, whilst for women it was a chance to experiment and many began to identify as bisexual (as Hite's early reports on her survey of women, carried out in the mid 70's, reveal). The openness about non-monogamy was nevertheless often perceived to be more positive than hiding it – for instance conflicts within a 'V' arrangement could now be openly discussed and negotiated in a way which could not have occurred a few years previously.

Although only a small remnant of the commune movement still exists today, relationship patterns have become more diverse in the US. In 1992 for example there were 3 million cohabiting unmarried male/female couples, as opposed to 0.5 million in 1970. Domestic partnerships are now legally codified in San Francisco and New York (although this can be merely viewed as the state adapting its control mechanisms in response to the failure of previous mechanisms). In a survey of 1200 people in 1990 by the Massachusetts Mutual Life Insurance Company, 75% of respondents gave their definition of family as "a group of people who love and care for each other", in preference to more conventional definitions (Diamond, 1992). Surveys of extra-marital sex in the US have given percentage figures from 36% to 71% of men, and 21% to 57% of women that had ever experienced it (Diamond, 1992: 154). Other surveys showed that 4% of 3880 married people thought that open marriage was possible, and that 1.5% of married couples practised swinging (the corresponding figure for Japan was 0.3%).

The lesbian and gay liberation movement of the late sixties set out to 'smash monogamy' along with other conventions of capitalism. Lesbians and gays who tried to imitate heterosexual norms of marriage and couplehood were regarded as oppressing themselves and in need of having their awareness raised (Altman, 1994). These principles were soon replaced however with campaigns for the right to 'gay marriages' and these were successful in Norway, Sweden and other European countries (Saalfield, 1993). To an extent social pressures work against the stability of gay or lesbian relationships (eg, married bisexual men who are forced to limit their gay relationships to covert and transitory casual sex), so that non-monogamy in lesbian and gay communities is not entirely a positive choice. However, there is also a greater acceptance of relationship diversity in these communities, and more flexibility in relationship patterns. Sex often occurs between friends for example in the gay male community, and lesbians may maintain friendships with ex-lovers to a much greater extent than happens in the heterosexual world (Becker, 1988).

## 9.4 The Future

A wide variety of models for organising non-monogamous relationships now exist and have been successfully applied. These include triads, polyfidelity (non-monogamous groups closed to sexual relationships outside the group), 'line marriages', open marriages and distributed commitment. Traditionally non-monogamy has been seen as a way by which men can exploit women, and as something which women should object to (and it has certainly been exploitative in a number of patriarchal societies). In the Wellcome survey for example, women were consistently more opposed to non-monogamy than men. However in some ways non-monogamous relationships can be more balanced in terms of power, since the participants will not be completely dependent on a single person, and there is thus less scope for abuse or violence. Often it is the women in such relationships who have more options than the men, since they will have, for demographic reasons, more possibilities of other relationships. Evidence from recent research into 'swinging' (Dixon, 1985) has shown that many women actually gain in self-confidence and self-realisation from this activity, which has been conventionally seen as something imposed on them.

Non-monogamous relationships could also redefine the power structures within the family which lead to children being treated as the exclusive property of their parents. Care for children could be given by any of the adults within a relationship, on the basis of convenience and inclination, rather than being the sole responsibility of the biological parents. Since the family is in many ways the model for other power structures within society, this could have a significant impact on these structures.

Non-monogamy could help to break down the atomised and isolating nature of present Western society, organised around family units and couples, and excluding those who fall outside of such units. Ideally it should be possible for there to be a continuum between friendship and sexual relationships, with the details of particular arrangements determined by the individuals involved, not by legal or conventional constraints. These associations could challenge the implications of exclusive 'ownership' which are part of most sexual relationships in our society. They could redefine sexual acts to be more concerned with a general sensuality and eroticism rather than being genitally focussed. Instead of sexual acts taking place in a fixed framework of roles and expectations (breadwinner versus housewife/financial versus emotional support), they would be a negotiated choice between individuals, each of whom would (hopefully) be enhanced by the association.

# Chapter 10

# Liberty in Chains: The Diaries of Anne Lister (1817–24)

**Emma Donoghue**

'Non-monogamy' has a modern ring to it, which can be misleading; this debate is nothing new. For instance, the first volume of the diaries in which Anne Lister (1791–1840) recorded her daily life in secret code offers fascinating evidence on multiple sexual and romantic connections among a group of friends in Regency Yorkshire[1].

To offer a resume of Anne Lister's love-life over even the eight years covered in the first volume of the published journals is far from easy. Only one thing is simple, her exclusive romantic and sexual commitment to women. 'I love, and only love, the fairer sex,' Lister wrote; 'my heart revolts from any other love than theirs.' (29/1/1821)

Historians are only now beginning to piece together a map of the complex changes in the way sexuality (as we call it now) has been viewed over the past few centuries. It is true that Lister's era had no agreed concept of a single lesbian identity, but (contrary to what most dictionaries suggest) it did have plenty of words for same-sex relationships and tendencies. 'Romantic friendship', in which passion between women was expressed only above the waist, was still generally praised in English society at this time; the suspicions occasionally levelled at men who loved each other rarely touched women, who were generally seen as sexless. But if Anne Lister's acquaintances had realised the truth about what she did in bed, they could have called her a 'tribade', a 'hermaphrodite', a 'Lesbian', a 'woman-lover', a 'lover of her own sex', a 'tommy', or (most likely, at her social level) a 'Sapphist'[2]. Being a lover of your own sex was seen by some people as a bar to marriage, but by others as an extra, a harmless hobby or spare-time vice[3]. Anne Lister saw herself as so 'mannish' and so exclusively devoted to women that she would never marry, whilst many of her lovers did.

But Lister's feelings for different women are much harder to categorise than her sexual orientation. After a boarding-school affair with Eliza Raine (who became mentally ill), Lister's first adult lover seems to have been a woman six years older, Isabella Norcliffe (sometimes known as Tib). In 1812, Tib had introduced Lister to Marianne Belcombe, who became the love of her life. Though Tib was never the focus again, she and Anne remained lovers, on and off, and Tib clung to hopes of a future commitment.

In 1815 Marianne married Charles Lawton, a wealthy landowner nineteen years her elder. Although during the previous century the idea of choosing a marriage partner for reasons of personal taste and affection had taken over from the concept of marriage for family interest, a prospective bride was still supposed to weigh all the factors (money, social status, character), rather than acting on romantic impulse[4]. Marianne's main motive was financial security. The marriage was Anne's idea originally – not yet having inherited Shibden Hall from her uncle, she could not afford to offer Marianne an income or a home – but she was shocked when Marianne went through with such a cold-blooded decision. This incident shows the clashing ideals of eighteenth-century sensibleness and Romantic self-fulfillment; for a woman as modern as Anne Lister, marrying without love was a sickening idea.

Charles Lawton's version of irresponsible non-monogamy was typical of men of his class: he seems to have seduced every maid he could get his hands on, which distressed Marianne but was not seen as unacceptable by the standards of the day. A wife, on the other hand, was meant to be totally faithful to her husband. But behind the mask of their respectable 'romantic friendship', Anne and Marianne remained lovers, writing regularly and snatching visits; their hope was that Lawton would die relatively young and they could set up home together. They kept their relationship a secret from everyone but a few close friends, including Marianne's four sisters (Lou, Eli, Harriet, and Nantz) – each of whom Anne eventually slept with, without telling Marianne. Anne flirted with many other women, and spent the

*Liberty in Chains*  81

years 1817 and 1818 infatuated with Miss Browne, but never got to the point of seducing her, partly because Miss Browne was her social inferior, partly because she soon got engaged to be married. 'She is in love, it seems, & this gives me little hope of making much impression on her in the amatory way,' Anne commented resignedly (30/1/19), accepting that not everyone was quite as flexible in these matters as she was.

An analysis of the way Lister recorded these overlapping relationships brings up most of the same issues as we struggle with today. But she used an odd mixture of the vocabularies of marriage, religion, seduction, and friendship. This points to the most important fact about Anne Lister's love life; she was a lesbian in a schizoid era when lesbians could be seen as anything from sinful pseudo-men to the most virtuous of women, and accordingly she needed several different vocabularies to describe her life.

Anne Lister claimed to be seeking always for a lifelong partner, longing for the time when she and Marianne (or Tib, sometimes) would finally 'get together' (28/5/17, 16/6/17). Sometimes the emphasis was on emotion – her need for a 'kindred spirit' (4/9/19) or 'some female companion whom I could love & depend on' (11/7/17) – and sometimes on finding a wife with suitable skills, fortune and social connections, to help her run Shibden Hall (10/8/19, 30/10/19, 12/6/24). Tib was very pragmatic, offering a variety of non-monogamous arrangements; since she was committed to living with her sister for at least half the year, she suggested to Anne 'I can visit you six months & the other six, you can get somebody else.' (10/7/19, 15/2/22).

But in fact Anne made most of her decisions based on passion, not reason. Over the years covered in the first volume, her interest in sleeping with Tib dwindled (especially as Tib took more snuff and wine and grew fatter); her great romantic object was usually Marianne. She often described commitment in the metaphor of owning someone's heart: 'I believe M_'s heart is all my own' (26/12/17, 17/2/20). A less possessive metaphor was one of linking: she wrote of Marianne 'Our hearts are mutually & entirely attached' (6/1/22).

The main model for pair bonds was, of course, heterosexual marriage. Much as Anne Lister resented it, she imitated it, to make her relationships sound valid. From the language of heterosexual courtship she borrowed the terminology (and rules) of vows, for example when she told Marianne 'Is there, or can there be any engagement at present? Was not every obligation on my part cancelled by your marriage?' (18/11/19, 30/8/20, 23/7/21). Every now and then, she and Marianne used to reaffirm their bond, calling each other 'husband' and 'wife' respectively – never swapping the roles (7/6/20). At times they even imitated civil marriage ceremonies: feeling close after some particularly good sex ('kisses') in July 1821, Anne recorded that they had 'bound ourselves to each other by an irrevocable promise for ever, in pledge of which, turned on her finger I gave her several years ago & also her wedding ring' (23/7/21). As well as co-opting the Lawton ring, Anne and Marianne planned to 'solemnise our promise of mutual faith by taking the sacrament together' using the Anglican sacrament of Holy Communion as a secret and silent wedding (28/7/21). But God rarely appears in the Lister diaries; his commands are heard only through the voice of social convention.

No matter how often Anne Lister claimed to be looking for a life partner, that was not all she wanted. Sometimes she realised that no single woman could give her all she wanted (20/7/23, 28/9/23). Until the faraway day when she and Marianne would be freed by Lawton's death and Lister's inheritance to 'get together' for good at Shibden Hall, Anne seems to have felt no real obligation to be monogamous. She was attracted to many other women; on one evening she spent half an hour in each of three women's bedrooms (Nantz Belcombe, Harriet Belcombe Milne, and Miss Vallance), making each jealous of the others (22/12/20). But it was only very occasionally that she actually had sex with anyone but her regular lovers, Marianne and Isabella. Perhaps because seducing someone new left her vulnerable to exposure (if they panicked, or wanted to punish her), Lister mostly stage-managed her flirtations up to (but stopping short of) the point of actual seduction. She often fantasised about maidservants, but does not seem to have actually seduced any in true lord-of-the-manor style (3/5/20, 27/2/23, 24/7/23). It may be that she was less interested in sex than in power; she gloated over the potential for seduction rather than seduction itself. For instance, she was not attracted to her friend Miss Pickford, another mannish lesbian like herself, but she still wondered 'It is very odd, but if I tried, would it be possible to make her melt at all?' (1/9/23).

Lister does not seem to have felt guilty about being a lesbian as such – she considered sex, justified by affection, to be less of a sin than masturbation (5/8/23). But sometimes she felt rather bad about all these interests in other women, referring to them as her 'foolishness' (28/8/94, 13/5/18), 'making a fool of' another woman (8/4/23, 11/7/23), or getting into a 'scrape' (18/2/19, 12/3/23). The terms are those of schoolgirl naughtiness, minimising her sense of guilt. Sometimes she told Marianne of feeling specifically religious remorse about sleeping with her as she was 'another man's wife'; this was 'adultery', which only the two women's 'prior connection' could excuse (31/8/18, 18/11/19, 20/8/23). But these conversations can also be read as her attempt to make Marianne feel guilty. This idea that one could justifiably carry on 'prior connections' allowed her to keep sleeping with Isabella with Marianne's full knowledge. Someone new, and more alluring, would be considered much more of a betrayal, so Anne never told Marianne about her new lovers.

It is interesting that Isabella, who seems to have had no other lover but Anne at this time, was all in favour of non-monogamy (1/8/19). For instance, at a time when she felt solidly committed to Marianne in 1822, Anne claimed not to want to sleep with Marianne's sister Eliza Belcombe since 'I was much altered of late in all these matters'. But Isabella responded mockingly 'It would be unnatural in you to not like sleeping with a pretty girl' (28/1/22). Isabella's attitude can be explained in two ways: she had nothing to lose from Anne's wanderings, since she was never going to be Anne's focus, and it is also easy to deduce that she wanted to undermine Anne's primary commitment to Marianne.

Most of the time, Anne Lister recorded no guilt at all in her flippant pursuit of sexual freedom. Her androgynous gender identity allowed her to take advantage of the double standard which has traditionally made having multiple sexual partners a male privilege; she seems to have felt that, as the 'husband', she had rights that she would never have allowed to the 'wife', Marianne. In true rake style, she referred to her early affairs as 'adventures' (19/12/17), and 'intrigues' (18/6/24), or sowing her 'wild oats' (20/8/23). Sometimes she expressed complete contempt for the other woman: she wrote of Nantz Belcombe, 'I believe I could have her again in spite of all she says, if I chose to take the trouble' (5/12/20, also 8/4/23).

Besides heterosexual models, another influential model for love relationships between women was romantic friendship. This was not meant to be exclusive – if you loved your friend, you would delight in her loving others too – nor troubled by jealousy. Anne often told her friends that she felt 'different things' for different people (28/8/17, 3/3/19, 6/10/23), so she could have room for all in her heart (16/8/18). So in one vocabulary the heart is entirely owned; in another, it is a container for other hearts, what Anne called 'the most convenient, capacious, concern possible' (9/4/19).

But barely-stifled jealousy did keep cropping up between friends, and particularly between lovers. Isabella tried to stay calm and reasonable, claiming to 'like [Marianne] as much as ever' (27/11/22) but the odd 'little tiff' or 'sparring conversation' revealed her as 'perpetually jealous' of Anne's much more loving treatment of Marianne (18/3/20, 15/2/22). Marianne occasionally admitted to being 'jealous' when she saw Anne flirting with Lou (18/12/17) and with Harriet (9/2/20), which Anne found flattering. Hearing that Marianne was, for once, 'unhinged' by the news that Tib was paying a visit. Anne commented merrily 'This looks like jealousy & as if she loved me' (27/6/19). So although life was simpler if no-one got possessive or jealous, Lister rather enjoyed being the focus of everyone's passionate attention and playing them off against each other.

Considering the potential for melodrama in such a complex storyline, there were surprisingly few big scenes. Compromise is usually the key-note. At the end of a quarrel with Isabella, Anne

> persisted that she did not suit & it was best to be candid at once. She cried a little & said she was very unhappy. I bade her cheer up & said there was no reason why we should not always be very good friends. She could not bear me to talk so. However, I gave her a kiss or two & we got the time over till twelve (18/3/22).

Marianne was rather more adept at matching Anne's manipulations with strategies of her own. She never tried to make Anne entirely monogamous, trying instead to keep the Lister libido in safe channels:

> M_ said, very sweetly & with tears at the bare thought she could never bear me to do anything wrong with ... anyone in my own rank of life. She could bear it better with an inferior, where the danger of her being supplanted could not be so great (3/4/20).

If Marianne could not entirely possess Anne's 'capacious' heart, at least she could be queen bee: 'As long, my dear Fred,' she wrote to Anne with the usual pet name, 'as I reign undisturbed over your heart, I am satisfied' (17/4/19). Occasionally she hinted a threat of withdrawing sexual privileges: 'M_ said, after we had got into bed, that if she did not believe me bound to her in heart as much as any promise could bind me, she should not think it right & certainly would not kiss me' (5/5/20). Marianne also used her position as 'wife': 'Sat up lovemaking, she conjuring me to be faithful, to consider myself as married, & always to act to other women as if I was M_'s husband' (10–13/5/20). The irony being, of course, that Marianne's real husband, Charles Lawton, was unfaithful in the extreme, so invoking the conventions of heterosexual marriage rang rather hollow.

It it hard to assess these relationships when we only have the diaries of one of the lovers. For example, did the others lie the way Anne did? It is not hard to deduce that by secretly bedding all the Belcombe girls, she was revenging herself on Marianne for getting married, but that does not explain her habitual deception of others. She referred to 'the deceiving game I was now obliged to play' to spare Isabella's feelings by not dashing her persistent hope that they would get together in the end, but really the feelings being spared were Anne's (18/11/20, 28/1/22). Similarly, having caught a 'venereal disease' from Lawton via Marianne, Anne kept it a secret from Tib, and passed it on through carelessness (2/11/23). One way of understanding all this is that the closet in which she was forced to live had trained Anne Lister in deception; only in her coded diary could she risk full honesty.

Lister was a terrible hypocrite: a casual reference to Nantz Belcombe 'whom I easily persuaded to sleep with me' (8/1/21) is followed a month later by a self-pitying letter to Marianne: 'You cannot doubt the love of one who has waited for you so long & patiently' (8/2/21). After getting a love letter from Nantz a few days later, Anne confided to her diary 'I shall not think much about her but get out of the scrape as well as I can, sorry & remorseful to have been in it at all. Heaven forgive me, & may M_ never know it' (12/2/21). Lister's part-time conscience did little to impel her towards living a more honest life.

But in her favour it should be said that as the secret and isolated lover of a married woman, Anne Lister felt powerless and frustrated from the start. Living together was only available to the exceptionally fortunate couple such as the legendary Ladies of Llangollen who shared bed and board for half a century in rural Wales, where Lister visited them (23/7/22, 3/8/22). So it is hard to tell whether Anne

Lister lived a non-monogamous life by inclination or on principle, or whether she was merely making the best of a bad lot. She often insisted in her diary that she was helpless in the face of circumstances: 'If I had M_ I should be very different', she claimed, and would 'want no more than her' (12/6/21). There is some truth in this; Anne's loneliness in months of enforced separation certainly drove her towards other women. But it is hard to believe that even if she had settled in rural Wales with Marianne, her imagination would not have kept roving.

Sometimes Lister waxed lyrical about their pseudo-marriage: 'Liberty & wavering made us both wretched ... The chain is golden & shared with M_, I love it better than any liberty' (13/6/21). But at other times she speculated that if she met someone better she would regret being 'tied' (15/2/23). In the Lister diaries, as in most of our own lives, we find the constant dilemma between the apparent security of monogamous commitment and the freedom and risks of non-monogamy.

# Notes

[1] All my references are taken from Helena Whitbread, ed. *I Know My Own Heart: the Diaries [1817-24] of Anne Lister (1791-1840)* (London: Virago, 1988; New York: New York University Press, 1994). The second (and even more gripping) volume published by Helena Whitbread is *No Priest but Love: the Journals of Anne Lister from 1824-1826* (Otley, West Yorkshire: Smith Settle, 1992; New York: New York University Press, 1994)

[2] See my *Passions Between Women: British Lesbian Culture 1668-1801* (London: Scarlet Press, 1993), pp. 2-7

[3] *Passions Between Women*, pp. 121-30

[4] Lawrence Stone, *The Family, Sex and Marriage in England. 1500-1800* (London: Weidenfeld and Nicolson, 1977), p. 273

# Chapter 11

# Clearly God Intended Polemics to be Threadbare: Some Christian Theological Justifications for Monogamy and Polygyny

**Jennifer Rycenga, San Jose State University**

Radical social movements are often tempted to establish a lineage, to look to the past for honourable forerunners as a step toward self-legitimation. Recent examples include the feminist search for a prepatriarchal epoch, and research on the history of les-bi-gays. However, such projects are not always helpful, and they may land us in ethical or perspectival quagmires. Such is the case for contemporary people living outside of a strictly monogamic system. While there are many historical precedents for polygamy, polygyny, polyandry, and other forms of non-monogamy, the historic reasons and explanations for these forms cannot be carried into our time, and raise serious questions about the self-serving nature of social-sexual justifications.

When I first undertook to examine the nature of theological justifications for polygamous and monogamous modes of sexual relating, I admit that I had a strong bias, as a feminist theorist of religion, that men in positions of power would arrange the world to their liking and their needs, and then impute their ideas to the authority of God. Though I hoped that this initial view would yield to greater complexities, the history is such that I do not need to add nuances to my original thesis, so much as to dress it up in its own grotesque costuming. Precautionary critiques emerge: that the symbiotic relationship between theological speculation and social ordering makes any appeal to divine authority dangerous, and that it is far too simple for these apologetic, justificatory mechanisms to elide questions of freedom, spirituality and subjectivity. By placing form above content, the monogamists and polygamists of the past glorified the social constraints of marriage and effectively erased the love and responsibility of human inter-relationship.

## 11.1 Religion and Relating

Marriage and similar socially legitimated forms of sexual relating have been constructed and administered by men, largely to serve what are perceived as male needs.[1] These needs include knowledge of paternity, proof of sexual prowess, property management and inheritance, and the effective domestic mirroring of public or religious structures of authority. This means that even public debates over the preference of monogamy or polygamy have been conducted between men, usually in ways which have, at worst, trampled women's subjectivity, or, at best, treated women's lives as secondary to the principal issues.[2]

From the earliest Neolithic artifacts which exaggerate the secondary sexual characteristics of women/goddesses,[3] to the monotonous droning of the religious right-wing against all developments in reproductive and sexual freedom, human sexual relations have almost invariably been interpreted within a religious framework. There are many reasons for this. Given that religion invariably ascribes meaning, the magnetic import of life-cycle events such as birth, coming-of-age, and sexual drive have elicited ritualisation and interpretation within religious world-views. Individual religious traditions, being concerned with their own continuity between generations and over time, have encouraged – and even rendered mandatory – reproductive modes of heterosexuality and standard forms of family structure.[4] Similarly, since religious mythology has long been concerned with cosmogonic issues, sexuality has been understood to replicate the creative activities and energies that shaped the world.[5] Religion has also been obsessed with power:[6] since sexual experiences and feelings are among the most intense in human lives, the need to understand, control, utilise, or banish this mode of power underlines a great deal of religious/sexual history.

Theological justifications for social/sexual systems are often direct reinforcements of socially restrictive sexual systems. This is patently obvious in the absurdity of arguments against the ordination of women in the Catholic church, or in the limited literalism of the 'rib' arguments given below. However, there is a similar tendency among sexual radicals, reformers and revolutionaries to likewise understand their forms of sexual relating as having a spiritual component. Looking only at US history, numerous examples can be cited. The nineteenth century alone witnessed the Shakers' radical celibacy,[7] the group marriage and birth control exercised by the Perfectionist Oneida community,[8] the feminist principles of the Brook Farm experiment,[9] the mixture of free-love and spiritualism in the lives of Ezra and Angela Heywood and other anarchists,[10] and the Mormon advocacy of plural marriages.[11] All show a rethinking of the sacrality inherent in sexual relations and a willingness to re-evaluate the institution of marriage. Even in the twentieth century, when the material conditions of sexuality are so different from the past, many practitioners of non-traditional sexual relationships produce religious reasons for their activities. Prime among these are spiritual movements within the lesbian, gay, and bisexual liberation movements: the Radical Faeries,[12] feminist Wicca,[13] the Metropolitan Community Church,[14] the borderlands/mestiza philosophy of Gloria Anzaldúa,[15] gay native American spiritualities,[16] African-Caribbean traditions,[17] the explorations of gay and lesbian South Asians into queer aspects of the Hindu tradition,[18] and white radical lesbian-feminist thought.[19]

This essay, however, will deal with historical examples in which rationalisations were offered to justify compulsory monogamy or to recommend widespread polygyny.[20] Furthermore, these religious apologetics all too frequently reflect and reinforce prevailing attitudes of racism, sexism, and imperialism, and they all value social order above human freedom.

## 11.2 One God, One Wife

In most white and European-derived cultures, monogamous heterosexual marriage is officially authorised by the state and blessed by organised religious bodies. While the Hebrew Bible[21] has a number of prominent examples of polygyny – most notably the patriarchs Abraham and Jacob, and Kings Solomon and David – the authorities in both Rabbinic diaspora Judaism and the codified Christianity of the

Church Fathers are thoroughly (and polemically) monogamous. Their practical reasons include an obsession with marriage as the vehicle for procreation, a desire for purity and social control, and warding off the (feared) chaos of licentiousness. Within Christianity, this drive for purity leads to asceticism, anti-body attitudes, and an explicit misogyny.

One key theological pivot in favour of monogamy was its parallelism with monotheism – a shared principle of uniqueness.[22] For example, Tertullian states "We admit but one marriage, just as we recognise but one God."[23] The intertestamental, apocryphal Jewish literature draws analogies between marital monogamy, bodily purity, spirituality, and monotheism, and stresses that marital relations exist only for reasons of procreation.[24] The Wisdom of Solomon, ironically named after a polygynous king, polemically links non-monotheistic religions with non-monogamy and impurity:

> *the worship of idols not to be named is the beginning and cause and end of every evil ... .*
> *For whether they kill children in their initiations, or celebrate secret mysteries,*
> *or hold frenzied revels with strange customs,*
> *they no longer keep either their lives or their marriages pure,*
> *but they either treacherously kill one another, or grieve one another by adultery,*
> *and all is a raging riot of blood and murder, theft and deceit, corruption,*
> *faithfulness, tumult, perjury,*
> *confusion over what is good, sexual perversion,*
> *disorder in marriages, adultery and debauchery*
> (Wisdom of Solomon 14: 27, 23-26)[25]

Singularity of deity (monotheism) and singularity of a people's relation to that deity (exclusivism) are extrapolated to singularity in marriage. Multiplicity is cast as "disorder" and "debauchery." Christian thought draws from the particularity of the Christ-event in making similar claims for monogamy; thus, Paul's exhortation to married couples in Ephesians 5:22-33 draws the analogy: husband : wife :: Christ : Church, in which "the state of monogamy is exalted ... (and) used as a symbol of the relationship of Christ to the Church."[26]

However, continuity between monotheism and monogamy is logically inconsistent, since monotheism calls for *many* people to give fealty to *one* god. More seriously, monotheism carries severe exclusionary impulses, which carry over into monogamist arguments: "The counterpart of revelation is damnation of those who refuse to accept it."[27]

Christian monogamists have slid into an evolutionary, triumphalist model, which holds that Christianity is more advanced than other religions, and that monogamy is more 'advanced' than polygyny. Geoffrey Parrinder defines this viewpoint:

> Generally speaking, polygamous marriages have existed in the lower and middle stages of culture, less frequently, if at all, in the very lowest and in the highest stages of civilisation ... gradually, from the earlier polygamy, the Old Testament advances to a nobler ideal. Even in the early days, the existence of a chief wife was a dawning recognition of ideal monogamy ... Polygamy belongs to the barbaric stage of society.[28]

Unfortunately, Parrinder's views are intimately tied into his larger subject matter – Christian missionary efforts in Africa, where, especially with the growth of anti-colonialist feelings in the twentieth century, the issue of plural marriage was hotly debated.[29] Parrinder's religio-ethno-centrism, is obvious when he connects polygamy – a traditional African practice – with barbarism and primitivism. It also emerges as an overt religio-cultural imperialism:

> If Christianity is *to conquer* any part of the world today, it must seek to strengthen marital fidelity and the monogamic ideal.[30]

The principle of uniqueness common to both monotheism and monogamy becomes a battering ram of conformity when it moves from theological abstraction to blunt reality. As we will see again, the *form* of monogamy takes on much greater importance than the *quality*, or, significantly, the *spirituality* of the relation that occurs within human intimacy.

## 11.3 Back to the Beginning: Literalism and the Competing Rib Theories

The marked preference among theologians for abstract form reaches absurd proportions when they attempt to utilise imagery from the Genesis creation story. The three examples given below are from vastly different historic eras and situations, but the guiding logic is the same – the symbolism of Eden is taken to indicate God's intentions.

The certainty with which both the pro and con sides thus determine God's wishes is startling.

The early Church father, Tertullian (ca. 160-ca. 230), is a writer known for his extremism and misogyny.[31] On the issue of monogamy – linked in his mind with discussions of virginity, chastity, proper behaviour of women, Christian uniqueness, and prohibitions against divorce and re-marriage – he says:

> we do not reject the union of man and woman in marriage. It is an institution blessed by God for the reproduction of the human race. It was planned by Him for the purpose of populating the earth and to make provision for the propagation of mankind. Hence, it was permitted; but only once may it be contracted. For Adam was the only husband that Eve had and Eve was his only wife; one rib, one woman.[32] Similarly, he states that, on the creation of Eve "God fashioned *one* woman for man, taking only *one* of his ribs, even though he had many" (76).[33]

Tertullian implies that, because God chose to make woman out of Adam's rib, and therefore could have made multiple women (i.e. the raw material was present in Adam's multiple ribs), God's decision to create but one woman was an intentional symbolic gesture toward uniqueness in marriage.

Eighteen centuries later, Parrinder follows Tertullian's logic quite closely:

> The fact that the first human beings are represented as having been one man, with one wife, clearly sets up monogamy as the original intention of God for the human race. And this is the sense which was brought out so memorably by Jesus, and taken even further so as to restrict divorce. Monogamy is thus the normal marriage for men and women, in the state of purity.[34]

Like most pro-monogamous Biblically-based arguments, Parrinder must ignore contrary evidence, such as the legend of Lilith, or the plural wives of the kings of Israel.[35]

The Protestant Reformation, stressing close reading of the Bible, provoked discussion on issues of plural marriage, albeit in rarefied intellectual forums.[36] Many leading European intellectuals from the sixteenth through the nineteenth century were favourably disposed towards polygamy, including Bernardino Ochino, John Milton, Schopenhauer, and even, albeit with some reluctance, Martin Luther himself.[37] Johan Leyser (1631-1682) wrote prolifically in defence of polygamy, which he touted as a cure to many social ills; in a work cast as a dialogue between a monogamist and a polygamist, he outlines some of the advantages:

> M. ... women will never accept polygamy.
> P. (Indignantly) Did not God set men in authority over them? In any case, women will submit to it if properly indoctrinated. And look at all the sins that spring from monogamy. It drives women to arrogance and domination over men. What is even more serious, monogamy leads to onanism [by which Leyser means intercourse with sterile or pregnant women], abortion, infanticide, whoremongering and adultery. All these could be abolished if polygamy were admitted.[38]

One important theme – and a crucial subject in the arsenal of the polygamophiles – is raised in this example: the contrast between a legitimated polygyny, and the hypocrisy of monogamists engaged in *de facto* polygyny as adulterers and/or customers of prostitutes. Unfortunately, Leyser here illustrates his own biases toward male power far more than he conveys anything concerning divine intention, just as Parrinder's earlier remarks tell us more about European spiritual imperialism than about spirituality. Leyser is not alone in this: women's subjectivity is consistently denied, suppressed, or ridiculed within arguments for and against polygyny.[39]

Leyser's reading of Genesis inverts that of Tertullian:

> That polygamy is part of the divine plan is clear from the fact that God created woman for man from a man's rib. For, since there are several ribs, a man should obviously have several wives.[40]

Here, the logic implies that if God had intended for men to have but one wife, he would have created Eve from a singular, unique bone in Adam's anatomy. God's choice of the rib allows Leyser to extrapolate that multiple ribs means multiple wives.[41]

Aside from their unintentional humour, these examples of Biblical interpretation point to a continuity in Christian religious thought which eschews experimentation and spontaneity in human relations, and thinks instead in terms of hierarchy, tradition, and an inflexible image of how God's intentions (once determined) are meant to pattern the social structure of human relationships. What I find intriguing is how the body, sexuality, desire, and the spirituality resident in such experiences, is so consistently avoided. It would appear that Christianity's anti-somatic tendencies reinforced the social formalism of intimate relations, at least in writing. When you couple this formalism with the historical realities of racism, misogyny, homophobia, and religious imperialism, the results can lead to unattractive polemics on both sides.

## 11.4 A Peculiar People – the Mormon Experiment with Polygyny

[42] Joseph Smith (1805-1844), founder of the Mormons, created dissension among his followers during and after his lifetime by his adoption of 'celestial' marriage. This theology of plural marriage is elaborate and original, because the Mormon principle of continuous revelation allows for subtle shifts in argumentation and reaction to opposition. But no amount of revelation could offset the fiercely critical attacks from outside the church which were incited by plural marriage. The United States and various local political powers used every tactic they had, including a Supreme Court case,[43] absolute disenfranchisement,[44] and even military might to force the Mormons to surrender plural marriage. The arguments of the monogamists against the Mormons in the latter half of the nineteenth century were no more convincing or conclusive than those of their predecessors, but the tactics used to preserve the sanctity of the monogamic ideal, in the face of an actual community living an alternative form of marriage, were ruthless.

Unfortunately, the Mormon grounds for multiple marriage are similarly chilling. One of Joseph Smith's earliest musings on the topic (from 1831) concerned the need for white Mormon men to intermarry among native Americans. Smith hoped his followers marry "Lamanites and Nephites, that their posterity may become *white, delightsome and just.*"[45]. Smith also saw that adopting a doctrine of polygamy might make proselytizing in foreign lands easier.[46] When Smith's inner circle started to issue pro-polygyny propaganda, the theology was overtly patriarchal. Orson Pratt told Mormon women that if you lacked a husband in this life, you won't get one in the next life, and you will have nothing.[47] Just as Smith had addressed his white male followers, so Pratt tried to impress on white Mormon women their duty to endure childbirth for those eternal souls awaiting bodily form:

> The Lord has not kept them (eternal souls) waiting for
> five or six thousand years past, and kept them waiting
> for their bodies all this time to send them among the

Hottentots, the African negroes, the idolatrous Hindoos, or any other of the fallen nations that dwell upon the face of the earth.[48]

The revelations that Joseph Smith received concerning polygamy were tied to power, reproduction, and male supremacy. While it was the duty of men to have plural wives, if a woman were to be with more than one man, "she has committed adultery, and shall be destroyed; for they (women) are given unto him (man) to multiply and replenish the earth."[49]. The official church pronouncement that Pratt penned, issued August 29, 1852, explained that polygamy was not for the crass satisfaction of carnal desire, but for "numerous and faithful posterity,"[50] a position that would be vigorously maintained by later Mormon apologists.

The response from the outside world was immediate. The Democrats distanced themselves at once from the Mormons: Stephen Douglas condemned plural marriage even as he supported the continuation of slavery.[51] The newly-formed Republicans pledged themselves to fight the "twin barbarisms of slavery and polygamy" – a promise they kept, as they became the implacable foes of the Mormons in Utah and Idaho following the Civil War.[52] And even that weakest and most vacillating of leaders, President Buchanan, found the energy to send troops to Utah in the late 1850's.[53]

Predictably, such responses united the Mormons.[54] Since there was no explicit law against polygamy in 1852, the Mormon leadership foresaw that the issue would be decided in the courts, and hoped that principles of religious freedom would carry the day. Unfortunately, that was not the case. As B. Carmon Hardy points out, the Mormons were putting polygamy forward at a time when "romantic companionship and transformation of the home into an affective, sentimental nest was elevating monogamy to a near religion," and when Darwinian thought was applied to make monogamy appear as the most 'evolved' form.[55] Furthermore, Mormon polygamy, due to the confluence of the Republican campaign against it, the Darwinist racism of the day, and the over-determined nature of the Mormon's own theological bigotry, was trapped in the quagmire of America's psychosis concerning race:

> Soon after the 1852 announcement, the question of Mormon polygamy became entangled with that of slavery ... As part of his defence for plurality, Orson Pratt argued that Utah citizens be treated like those of the South, where local institutions were left to local control. Although Utah stood with the Union when war came, Brigham Young told Horace Greeley that he looked upon

> slavery as a divine institution, not to be abolished until "the curse pronounced upon Ham" was removed. Linkage was reinforced by non-Mormons who defended both institutions as approved by the scriptures. Contending that elevated society was dependent on them, Henry Charles Lea pleaded that Americans see the importance for every citizen having the liberty to possess "as many slaves as Abraham, and as many wives as Solomon."[56]

This racism doubled back upon the Mormons, as white journalists vilified them as a new race with genetic deformities,[57] "cast with blacks as animal and profligate."[58] And so the courts and legislatures came down unfavourably on the Mormons, in a battle that lasted from the 1852 declaration, past the official withdrawal of polygamy in 1890, and into the middle of the twentieth century.

Those who opposed the Mormons were not standing on pure moral grounds. Partisan politics behaved with its usual sordidness; since Mormons were almost unanimously Democrats, Republicans opposed their voting rights and the admission of any states that could conceivably have a Mormon majority.[59] And the defence of monogamy was based in Euro-American cultural hegemony and arrogance,[60] in combination with a very slippery slope argument – that Western civilisation depended on monogamy, and that any laxity in enforcing conformity would lead to moral decline. Hardy surmises that the Mormon's opponents'

> concern lay less with the sexual derelictions of individuals than a sense that the form of the monogamous home was threatened. The purpose of anti-polygamy laws was to expunge the 'semblance' of a competing non-monogamic order of home life. This is why, in the face of Mormon consternation, convictions for plural marriage were allowed even when no sexual relations between spouses existed. Replying to Mormon allegations of hypocrisy, that adulterers and prostitutes were allowed to vote under anti-polygamy laws while Mormons who married their companions were not, the Utah Commission restated Congress's purpose. They were attempting, said the commission, to meet what they saw as a conscious assault on "the most cherished institution of our civilisation – the monogamic system." If plural marriage were tolerated, the commission explained, it could spread and weaken monogamy, which, they repeated, was the most important reason for "the advancement of civilisation everywhere."[61]

## 11.5 Conclusions

Looking at these few historic examples from Christian traditions, theological justifications for modes of sexual relating have been a) promulgated by men, b) concerned more with social order than with personal subjectivity, and c) sport an argumentative, absolutist tone which d) discourages individual variation or social experimentation. The spirituality inherent in sexuality and human relationships is ignored in favour of the social utility of progeny, order, male dominance and authority. Furthermore, when it is overtly the *form* of marriage, rather than the *content*, that is the subject of the debate, both monogamists and polygamophiles share common assumptions about other parameters of social order, such as Christian superiority and compulsory heterosexuality.[62]

As contemporary discussions of new forms of relating arise, and are met by an increasingly conservative backlash, the tendency of this particular argument within Christianity to degenerate into illogical obstinacy and social formalism can be instructive. For instance, the unwillingness of the proponents of monogamy to allow for multiple forms of relating appears to be consistent in polemics across time. The pro-polygamists are usually more flexible, but rarely genuinely inclusive of sexual differences. The buttresses for pro-polygamy arguments have almost always emanated from social utility: more children, more wealth, demographic imbalances between men and women,[63] the so-called 'natural' polygyny of men, and so on.[64]

I am reminded of a pithy slogan: "Anyone who says that God is on their side is as dangerous as hell."[65] These self-righteous justifications, in the final analysis, do not represent spiritual and/or sexual experience. By making the move towards abstraction and social form, these writers entangled themselves in complex webs of injustice and power. The cautionary impulse emerging from this brief survey is that only a sweeping critique of the entire social system, including marriage, can consciously avoid replicating or condoning its least attractive aspects. It would be difficult for a contemporary non-monogamist to take unalloyed pride in the Mormon struggle, or in the writings of Leyser. While these historic examples give evidence that monogamy has not been intellectually monolithic in European or Euro-American history, they conversely demonstrate that racism, religio-cultural imperialism, and misogyny *have* been practically monolithic – hardly a promising foundation on which to build.

Voices have been heard, and are newly emerging, calling for the necessary radical changes to supplant the current limited forms of sexuality and sexual relating. Not surprisingly, many of those voices come from lesbian and gay experience, and from feminist analyses: from those people who have been most directly and negatively affected by the sex-gender-sexuality assumptions of previous ideologies.[66] The challenge remains: can the intuitive links between religion – where meaning is located and ascribed – and sexuality – where power, ecstasy, and joy are located – be maintained without devolving into apologetics?[67] Given the contemporary political situation, this is an urgent question for those who treasure the spiritual quest and human intimacy of sexuality.

*Clearly God Intended ...* 99

# Notes

[1] Other socially legitimated forms of sexual relating have included male-based de facto polygamy – the keeping of mistresses, the utilisation of prostitution, and so on. Of course, some cultures have explicitly sanctioned plural marriages. It is important to note that not all socially legitimated forms of sexual relating have been heterosexual – the example of Athenian homosexuality alone would be enough to disprove this. However, it is equally as important to note that, with the possible exception of Charles Fourier, and Aristophanes' passing mention of it in Plato's Symposium, no male theologians or philosophers have been eager to justify or validate female same-sex relations.

[2] For example, observe the limited suffrage given to women in Utah territory (Van Wagoner, 1989: 108 – 109), or the Christian monogamist-apologists' illustrative use of women's rights in their battles with African Christian polygamists (Parrinder, 1950: 35, 49). In both cases, women's issues were utilised by men to bolster the strength of arguments that assumed male privilege and dominance in the social order. In the Utah suffrage case, allowing women to vote – in a highly contested political space that intimately involved their own polygynous status – naturally *more* than doubled Mormon voting strength. Given that the Mormons at this time voted in a block, the adoption of women's suffrage in Utah territory can hardly be interpreted as an unalloyed progressive move. However, it is just as crucial to note historical contradictions: the compromise that engineered Utah's admission to the United States included the removal of the vote from women (Van Wagoner, 1989: 133), and that Eastern feminists did not support their Mormon sisters' enfranchisement (Arrington and Bitton, 1979: 179). In the African missionary case, any appeal to women's rights was a European culturally-bound one, that failed to take into consideration the not inconsiderable plight of multiple wives who were forcibly abandoned when their husbands converted to Christian ways, and failed to notice the woman-centered economic and community power that multiple wives might have.

[3] See the writings of Marija Gimbutas on Old European culture (Gimbutas, 1982, 1989).

[4] In some traditions, this has become an overt command. For instance, the Biblical injunction "Be fruitful and multiply" (Genesis 9:7) has played a significant role in pro-natalist theologies in both Judaism and Christianity. This Biblical passage was a crucial one to

the Protestant Reformers, and helped to usher in renewed theclogical discussion of polygyny (Cairncross, 1974: 2).

[5] On the hieros gamos, or 'sacred marriage', see (Feuerstein 1992: 57f); on Kabbalistic marriage symbolism, see (Scholem, 1946: 232).

[6] Gerardus van der Leeuw bases his phenomenology of religion on the concept of power; (van der Leeuw, 1967: passim).

[7] On the Shakers, see (Foster, 1991); (Kern, 1981); (Kitch, 1989); (Procter-Smith, 1985).

[8] On the Oneida community, see (Battan, 1988); (Dalsimer, 1975); (DeMaria, 1978); (Foster, 1991); (Kern, 1981).

[9] Joel Myerson has collected participant writings on the Brook-Farm community; see (Myerson, 1987).

[10] (Blatt, 1989).

[11] On the Mormons see (Arrington and Bitton, 1979); (Beecher and Anderson, 1987); (Bunker and Bitton, 1983); (Embry, 1987); (Hardy, 1992); (O'Dea, 1957); (Van Wagoner, 1989); (Young, 1954).

[12] See (Connor, 1993).

[13] See (Starhawk, 1979); (Adler, 1979).

[14] On the MCC Church see (Perry with Swicegood, 1990); (White, 1994); (Goss, 1993).

[15] (Anzaldúa, 1987).

[16] See (Paula Gunn Allen, 1986); (Roscoe, 1988); (Williams, 1986).

[17] On African-Caribbean traditions see (Brown, 1991); (Teish, 1985); (Lorde, 1982).

[18] On South Asian gay and lesbian experience, see (Ratti, 1993).

[19] See (Daly, 1984); (Grahn, 1984).

[20] Since the form of polygamy that was advocated by Christian figures is actually limited to one man having many wives, I will often use the technical form of 'polygyny' to describe this practice. However, in the original documents, the authors usually use the more generic 'polygamy'.

[21] The term "Hebrew Bible" is preferred to "Old Testament" in recognition of the autonomy of Judaism.

[22] For a particularly tortured example of the reasoning of singularity, Helander quotes Karl Barth: "In His choice and His covenant we meet not only the electing divine partner in His one-ness: the one Jahweh-Elohim, who can have no gods beside Him, Jesus Christ as the *one* mediator between God and men, the *one* Holy Ghost in the multitude of His Gifts. In this covenant also the created, the chosen partner, whether appearing as individual or as collective, always has the character of oneness; amongst all the nations Israel and only Israel, and in Israel Juda and only Juda, and in Juda the house of David exclusively, and in the house of David finally and lastly the one mysteriously planted progeny, the Son of Mary, and only He. And then likewise, not many congregations of the one Lord, but for all its divisions here and there, the *one* which is everywhere the same, the one Holy Catholic Church, besides which and outside which no one exists. And so the *one* Moses, the *one* Jeremiah, the *one* Peter, and also the *one* Judas, the *one* Paul, *this* judge, *this* prophet, *this* apostle and messenger for God, the *one* disciple Jesus loved; always chosen ones, from time to time, each in his place, each indispensable in his task, not exchangeable, not competing or subject to competition from anyone. Seen in the light of this choice and this covenant, marriage can only be monogamy." (47) As Helander wryly points out, with an argument like this "one can prove just about anything, e.g. that every family really should have only one child, or that each person should have only one friend." (Helander, 1958: 47).

[23] (Tertullian, 1956: 70).

[24] (Yarbrough, 1985: 10-11).

[25] New Oxford Annotated Bible with the Apocryphal / Deuterocanonical Books. ed. Bruce M. Metzger and Roland E. Murray. New revised Standard Edition. New York: Oxford University Press, 1991. p. 76-77. Yarbrough also cites how such an analogy was used specifically to repudiate male homosexuality, in the Sybilline Oracle: "But [the Jews] raise heavenwards holy hands, rising early from their bed and ever cleansing their flesh with water, and they honour Him alone who reigns forever, the Eternal, and after him their parents; and more than any men they are mindful of the purity of marriage. Nor do they hold unholy intercourse with boys, as do the Phoenicians, Egyptians, and Latins and spacious Hellas and many other nations of men, Per-

sians and Galatians and all Asia, transgressing the holy laws of the immortal God." (Yarbrough, 1985: 10)

[26] (Parrinder, 1950: 55). Of course, this analogy doesn't work; as Helander points out, "no immediate monogamic conclusion can be drawn. The congregation which is the bride of Christ, though being one, has many members. The body (whose head the husband is) consists of many limbs or members." (Helander, 1958: 41).

[27] (Cairncross, 1974: 8). One prominent contemporary exception to this exclusionary version of monogamy is found in the work of feminist writer Susan Dowell. While I find that her arguments for monogamy are personal, practical, and unconvincing, I appreciate that she doesn't need to create anti-polyfidelious libels or attacks to maintain her sense of what works for her. See (Dowell, 1987, 1990).

[28] (Parrinder, 1950: 5, 19, 35).

[29] Christian missionaries in Africa found themselves at a disadvantage vis-a-vis their Muslim counterparts on the question of polygamy. African intellectuals were quick to point out that the Christian proselytizers were more concerned about converting Africans to European customs than with assisting people spiritually. See (Dada, 1986); (Helander, 1958); (Hillman, 1975); (Parrinder, 1950).

[30] (Parrinder, 1950: 63). With similarly self-inflated superiority, Parrinder engages in an obvious case of Orientalism and then seeks to protect Judaism from charges of backsliding into polygynous relations when he cites Herod's polygamy as one of that king's "oriental vices" and then adds that Herod's faults don't matter, since he was "not a full-blooded Jew"!! (39-40). Compare this with Edward W. Said, Orientalism (New York: Vintage, 1978) and Howard Eilberg-Schwartz, The Savage in Judaism: An Anthropology of Israelite Religion and Ancient Judaism (Bloomington IN: Indiana University Press, 1990). Parrinder's later scholarly work, while not so explicit in its cultural imperialism, still fails to adequately discuss, let alone critique, the implications of proselytizing and other forms of religious oppression. See (Parrinder, 1984: 68) re. African traditional religions and progress, and 449–451 for a largely uncritical outline of Christian missionary history.

[31] For more analysis of Tertullian's thought and its relation to women, see (Torjesen, 1993); (Bray, 1979); (Timothy, 1973).

[32] (Tertullian, 1956).

[33] (Tertullian, 1956: 76).

[34] (Parrinder, 1950: 30).

[35] Parrinder dismisses the Lilith narratives as legends, (Parrinder, 1950: 30–31).

[36] There were also pressing political reasons for discussion of multiple marriages, as the marital/dynastic crises of Henry VIII of England and Philip the Magnanimous of Hesse provoked debate on the subject. See (Cairncross, 1974: 31f) on Philip's case, and 54f concerning Henry VIII.

[37] For more on all of these figures, see (Cairncross, 1974), and (Miller, 1974). It is also interesting to note that Milton knew, at least indirectly, of Ochino's work (Cairncross, 1974: 133-135), and that the early Mormons were familiar with similar writings by Martin Madan, dating from the 1730's (Hardy, 1992: 2, 85).

[38] (Cairncross, 1974: 77), parenthetical explanation his. Cairncross also addresses the question of Leyser's rabid misogyny (83).

[39] Polyandry was not debated by most Christian theologians; as a social form it never had much prevalence in Northern and Western European nations. One should not assume from this, however, that polyandry is always a woman-centered form, or a form respectful of women's sexuality and agency.

[40] (Cairncross, 1974: 80).

[41] After coming across these rib examples, I had a recurring picture of Adam, fragilely trying to protect his rib-less self against an angry band of women who realize that they can demobilise him with one good punch to his defenceless internal organs!

[42] The phrase "a peculiar people" was one the Mormons used to describe themselves (Van Wagoner, 1989: 102), (O'Dea, 1957)

[43] (Arrington and Bitton, 1979: 180).

[44] Merle Wells does an exceptional job of covering all aspects of the infamous Idaho Test-Oath; see (Wells, 1978). For a briefer account see (Blank, 1988: 56-57).

[45] Joseph Smith, quoted in (Van Wagoner, 1989: 3), emphasis mine. For those unfamiliar with the Book of Mormon, it maintains that the native Americans were Israelites, and that the Lamanites and Nephites faced each other in a dualistic battle, with the evil, darker-skinned Lamanites defeating the lighter-skinned Nephites and slaying their prophets. There are no actual North American tribes which call themselves by those names. For a Mormon childhood reminiscence about this story, see (Bailey, 1972: 51–57).

[46] (Van Wagoner, 1989: 51).

[47] (Van Wagoner, 1989: 47).

[48] Orson Pratt, quoted in (Hardy, 1992: 15).

[49] Joseph Smith, quoted in (van Wagoner, 1989: 56). Intra-Mormon tension over the polygamy issue played a role in Smith's destruction of the rival printing press in Nauvoo, Illinois, which led to his imprisonment and martyrdom in 1844; see (van Wagoner, 1989: 67-70), (Arrington and Bitton, 1979: 77-82).

[50] Pratt, quoted in (van Wagoner, 1989: 85). In this same document, Pratt cites Jesus' relationship with Mary, Martha and Mary Magdalen as a New Testament precedent for the Mormon marriage system (van Wagoner, 1989: 85)

[51] (van Wagoner, 1989: 86)

[52] (van Wagoner, 1989: 86), and (Wells, 1978: passim).

[53] (Arrington and Bitton, 1979: 165–170); (van Wagoner, 1989: 87–88).

[54] (van Wagoner, 1989: 102).

[55] (Hardy, 1992: 41–42).

[56] (Hardy, 1992: 39).

[57] (van Wagoner, 1989: 106)

[58] (Hardy, 1992: 41). There is also a sobering illustrated chapter on the racism of the anti-polygamists in Bunker and Bitton 1983, 75-94.

[59] (Wells, 1978), passim.

[60] Anti-polygamists consistently referred to Mormon polygamy as

Oriental; (Hardy, 1992: 41).

[61] (Hardy, 1992: 60), emphasis his

[62] This is true of some twentieth-century male advocates of polygamy; for instance, a book by Michael H. Brown, *The Case for Polygamy*, recycles many of the old Biblical arguments, along with an explicit dose of misogyny and homophobia. Who his audience was I do not know, as the book appears to have been self-published, but the invective includes blaming bisexual men (called 'fags' in the text) for disease, and saying that women want to be subordinate to men and will soon beg to have Biblical order restored!

[63] For instance, there was a temporary dispensation for men to have two wives, following the Thirty Years' War, and the Nazis were considering a similar action when battlefield losses mounted in World War II (Cairncross, 1974: 59, 212). Of course, this begs for a feminist analysis of male needs and power at the root of both war and social structures of compulsory gendered relationships.

[64] Mormon polygynists attacked monogamy as 'unnatural' (always a favorite word to use for one's sexual enemies!): "In a formal epistle from the First Presidency in 1885, traditional marriage practice was attacked as having 'dammed up' the natural channels God created for male sexual expression." (Hardy, 1992: 89)

[65] Button, private collection of author, purchased in Wall, South Dakota, USA, June 15, 1994.

[66] See for instance the works of (Fourier, 1967); (Brittain, 1929); (Hurcombe, 1987); (Hoagland, 1988); (Anzaldúa, 1987). An especially powerful new work of theology in relation to gay male non-monogamy is being developed by Kathy Rudy (Rudy, 1994), which circumvents many of the problems outlined in this paper. Rudy questions the monogamic ideal at the basis of community, suggesting that the diadic structure of monogamy leads people to give their "allegiance and commitment ... not to our larger community but to our partner or nuclear family" (6). She then speculates that so-called 'anonymous' gay male sex is actually a way of relating within a larger community.

[67] The question of apologetics is forefronted in the current debates about whether sexuality is genetic or chosen. When gays and lesbians say "I was born this way, I can't change, leave me be, etc." it sounds like a denial of agency, and therefore of creativity. But to maintain

that everyone deliberately, as an act of intellect, chooses their sexuality, is a blanket denial of bodily knowing. What is clear is that the rush to 'discover' a material genetic link is motivated by a short-term political desire to defuse the conservative Christian accusation that all gays and lesbians are 'sinners', and that the post-modern desire to claim that nothing is given naturally but everything is constructed is a philosophic move designed to defuse the false givenness of all modernisms, but without constructing anything in its place. Similarly, any attempt to say that monogamy, polygamy, heterosexuality or marriage are 'natural' would not be convincing; evidence from human communities and from the animal world is entirely inconclusive and contradictory. But to deny individual preference for one or the other system, or to say that such preference has no spiritual or metahuman significance, is once again a denial of non-rational and/or physically-based knowledge. Skirting such deadlocked arguments, and seeing how and why they are deadlocked, is one of the objectives that I hope the brief historical excursus of this article can achieve.

# Chapter 12

# Friends Can't be Lovers: The Paradox of Monogamy

**K. Lano**

Everyone has their own reasons for exploring or preferring non-monogamous options. For me, there seem to be two key advantages:

- freedom from expectations that I should "be everything" to a partner, that I fulfill all their needs and wants;
- the possibility of blending friendship and "serious" relationships.

The first is easy to explain – one of the strange things about modern Western society is the great expectations placed on relationships – that the two people involved should be able to meet each others emotional, sexual and intellectual needs, for years on end. What an intimidating prospect! This (unrealistic) set of expectations is a quite recent invention and is perhaps a product of our increasingly anonymous and alienating societies – in previous generations much wider networks of support (ie, extended families) were available, albeit with their own oppressiveness, and marriage was considered more prosaically functional (to raise children and to be economically productive).

The second is related to this. Present Western society has built up a strong division between the categories of 'friend' and 'lover', which, together with the above expectations, leads to us both imprisoning our partners and dis-empowering ourselves within intimate relationships.

This article will argue that the division between friends and lovers is another false dichotomy perpetuated by a society which intensively regulates sexuality and the forms of relationships, and should be contested.

## 12.1 Erotophobia and the Regulation of Sexuality

Sex has always been a highly problematic issue in Western societies. Recurrent 'moral panics' have arisen over the spread of syphilis, masturbation, homosexuality and AIDS, all featuring an undercurrent of revulsion and fear regarding sex. In part this may be due to the particular religious heritage of these societies, and perhaps to the more established nature of religious and state power structures, which attempt to try and control more and more of the lives of their subjects over time. In present society sex is one of the few areas of life which is not directly commodified – freely chosen sex between individuals is a non-consumerist pleasure, under the control of the individuals concerned, it makes no money for companies, and hence is redundant in capitalism except for its use in marketing money-earning products.

Often it seems that, in English culture in particular, people need to get stoned out of their heads on alcohol or drugs before they can get to the point of going to bed together. This could be seen as a way of denying sexuality or separating sexual behaviour from the rest of our lives, as a response to the religious and social teachings associating sexuality with guilt and disgust. A lot is done non-verbally, which is not a situation conducive either to the practice of safer sex or for genuine communication.

In the West self-sacrifice of personal interests and pleasures in favour of wage-slavery is still the norm: most employed people spend the vast majority of their waking hours either at work, travelling to and from work, or engaged in auxillary work activities. Any aspects of life outside work must be fitted into the moments unoccupied by this dominant activity. Sexuality is viewed by corporations as an unproductive distraction from the needs of the job – hence the continuing gender segregation of most forms of work, and the illegality of homosexuality in the armed forces. A better philosophy might be that work is a harmful distraction from sexuality.

Legally, it is still the case that there are many restrictions on which individuals can have sex, with these restrictions being consistently based on the principle that the only justification for sex is the possibility of reproduction. Thus, in the UK in 1994, heterosexual anal sex is still illegal (with a maximum penalty of life imprisonment), whilst rape in marriage has only recently become an offence. Male homosexual sex was made illegal and severely punished as it constituted a waste of sperm, whilst lesbian sex was ignored by the law.

Western societies are usually mass societies, in which individual pleasures and concerns are subordinated, and in which most of our daily interactions are with relative strangers. Pair bond relationships become seen as a means of temporary escape from the competitive and alienating nature of the rest of life, and become heavily weighted with expectations that they should serve to compensate for this, and provide, particularly for men, an opportunity for intimacy and significant communication. A strong separation is set up between 'serious' relationships and all other forms of interaction.

Thus Western societies are pervaded by a concern to restrict the scope of sexual feelings and behaviour, ideally to a purely reproductive context, or to conventional monogamous heterosexual couples of the same race and class. Blurring the boundaries between friendship and sexuality, and breaking the link between a sexual relationship and exclusive ownership of the partners by each other, is necessarily a challenge to the Western social codes.

## 12.2 Gender Polarisation

Surveys of women (Hodgekinson, 1986) consistently show that they rate 'being a best friend' as being of prime importance in a sexual partner, however this is perhaps more a reflection of what women feel they are *lacking* in their sexual relationships, and what they most feel in need of, rather than being a characteristic of their present relationships.

It may be that the conventional male-female partnership has a poor level of communication because of the stake which each partner has in the other, in their expectations of each other to act out restricted, well-defined roles within the relationship (economic support versus emotional support, mother and housewife). Thus anything which could disrupt this pattern, or lead to a questioning of it, becomes a threat. In addition, men and women are still brought up to find attractive quite gender-stereotyped and polarised characteristics: at some level women still expect men to be more assertive, to take the initiative, to be more successful, and so forth (in the UK the woman is the higher earner in only 2% of male-female couples – this is less a consequence of wage differentials than a clear selection decision of the couple themselves to choose a higher or lower earning partner respectively). Men that are conventionally attractive to women are often exactly the type of men who are not able to communicate well or act in an egalitarian way within a sustained relationship – they have become successful and hence visible to women through suppressing their own feelings in favour of an overriding commitment to work, to competition and a focus on status, tasks and achievements (Farrell, 1990). They may be sensitive to signs of weakness in an opponent, or to signs of a commercial opportunity, but not to the subtleties of their partner's emotional needs.

Amongst gay men there seems to be far less of a distinction between sexual relationships and friendships: sex can occur in a relatively relaxed manner between two friends without changing the entire meaning of the association as it does between men and women (one man does not suddenly expect the other to stay home and cook all his meals ...). One of the main differences between gay male partnerships and straight partnerships is over exclusivity: the expectation of exclusivity declines rapidly in gay male couples after the first year (Diamond, 1992), whilst for heterosexual couples it usually remains (unrealistically) high. Lesbians also seem less concerned about exclusivity and ownership than their straight counterparts, with over 50% of lesbians having participated in group sex in some surveys (Simenauer, 1982: 199).

These differences arise in part because of the relative lack of power differentials within same-sex relationships, and because these are not institutionalised and regulated by social expectations to the same degree as male/female relationships: thus it may be easier for same-sex pairings to define an individual meaning for their relationship, and to be more flexible in its operation. For similar reasons women may actually find close friendships more valuable than sexual relationships, given the power imbalances in the latter, and so have a definite motivation to ensure that a friendship does not become 'lost' through becoming sexual.

Heterosexual men and women still tend to have quite polarised attitudes to friendship and sexuality: such men are typically very strongly concerned to exclude any element of sexual attraction from their friendships with other men. Such 'friendships' in any case are often extremely superficial, based on functional rather than personal motivations (ie: they associate with someone only for the sake of their career or status) (Farrel, 1990). In their associations with women however, they expect far more in terms of emotional support, and allow themselves much stronger feelings, which, however, they identify with (sexual) love. To them, any female friend is a potential sexual partner. (They may not actually express these feelings because they know that they would not be acceptable to the woman, leading to an end of the friendship by her, or to a withdrawal from the relationship on his part, because to continue after a rejection of their sexuality would be too painful.)

Men may seem obsessed about sex, but this is only because to them, sex is their one means of being fully human, of achieving a deep connection with another person, being intimate and expressing feelings of affection and love which are otherwise suppressed and discouraged in the remainder of their lives.

In contrast women have been brought up to suppress their sexual feelings, but to be more emotionally expressive and communicative. Same-sex friendships can therefore be closer for women than for men (since sexual implications are more inconceivable), but relationships with men are divided into two exclusive categories: lovers versus friends, in which the woman may behave in very different ways (indeed in a sexual relationship with a man she may find herself adapting to fit his image and expectations of her, to become almost a different person). Thus in friendships between men and women, men generally wish to express feelings of affection and 'love' via physical intimacy, whilst women will seek any possible alternative to the sexual expression of feelings.

According to the conventional model of relationships then, the key distinction between friendship and sexual relationships are that the latter (between men and women) are central to the identity and indeed survival of the partners (married men have half the rate of suicide attempts than single men, and their other health indicators are usually better as well (Faludi, 1990)). Such a relationship validates the partners as 'real men' and 'real women' within society, and internally it seems to the participants to be a way in which their 'other half' can supply abilities which they themselves are lacking (due to gendered upbringing, rather than intrinsic inability).

'Love' might also be thought to be a significant difference between friendship and relationships, but this is not so. The feelings we term 'love' are perhaps no more than a (frequently deluded) hope that we have found a person who can 'complete' us in the above sense, who can solve the problems of our life and rescue us from the isolation and alienation of this society. More generally 'love' may be a means of pretending that we are not driven by sexual desires (love is not a central issue in who sleeps with who amongst gay men — the primacy of lust is generally acknowledged). Strong feelings of affection and appreciation are a part of many friendships — in different circumstances these feelings would be called 'love'.

If the present gender polarisation was reduced, so that men and women expected quite similar things from each other, and could avoid power imbalances in their relationships, then indeed it would be possible for the barriers between the categories of friend and lover to be reduced. New forms of association between men and women could be developed, closer to forms which have arisen in the lesbian and gay communities. Thus it would be possible for friends to occasionally sleep together when it seemed appropriate, but without either believing that they 'owned' the other, or could expect sex or other services as a right. Instead the form of the relationship could be mutually negotiated to meet each others needs and other commitments.

This is not to assert that the overlap between friendship and sexuality will be completely unproblematic. Even in a context where individuals are out to their partners as non-monogamous, there can still be feelings of betrayal or jealousy if an association which was assumed to be 'just a friendship' suddenly becomes something more. This is perhaps one of the reasons why polyfidelitous arrangements disallow such new relationships outside the group: the disruption caused by the change could lead to a breakdown of the established arrangement. The attitude taken in some 60's communes, a completely laissez-faire approach in which individuals considered that it was their business alone what new relationships they formed, and not a point of discussion with any existing partner(s), seemed in particular to lead to hurt feelings and conflict. Some prior discussion and negotiation with existing partner(s) would seem at least polite!

## 12.3 Conclusions

This article has identified two key reasons why 'friends cannot be lovers': the conventional polarised conditionings of men and women, and the erotophobic and isolated nature of Western societies. Together these lead to male-female relationships being charged with a weight of expectations and functions which prevent good communication: they only enhance the partners lives to the extent that they enable them to obtain social validation for living up to their expected behaviour. In contrast, friendships are generally more egalitarian and flexible, but are themselves damaged by fears of sexual implications.

# Bibliography

[1] Adams, Mary Louise (1989). "There's No Place Like Home: On The Place of Identity in Feminist Politics". FEMINIST REVIEW 31:22-23.

[2] Adler, Margot (1979). DRAWING DOWN THE MOON: Witches, Druids, Goddess-Worshippers, and other Pagans in America Today. Boston: Beacon Press.

[3] Allen, Paula Gunn (1986). THE SACRED HOOP: Recovering the Feminine in American Indian Traditions. Boston: Beacon Press.

[4] Anapol, Deborah (1992). LOVE WITHOUT LIMITS: THE QUEST FOR SUSTAINABLE INTIMATE RELATIONSHIPS. San Rafael, California: Intinet Resource Center.

[5] Angelico, Teresa (1989). "In Search of 'Wholeness'" DIVERSITY 7(1)

[6] ANSLIM (1992). BEYOND SEXUALITY. London, UK: Phoenix Press.

[7] Anzaldúa, Gloria (1987). BORDERLANDS/LA FRONTERA: The New Mestiza. San Francisco: Aunt Lute.

[8] Bailey, Paul (1972). POLYGAMY WAS BETTER THAN MONOTONY: to my grandfathers and their plural wives. Los Angeles: Westernlore Press.

[9] Baker, Karin (1992). "Bisexual Feminist Politics: Because Bisexuality is Not Enough" in E.R. Weise (ed) CLOSER TO HOME: BISEXUALITY AND FEMINISM. Seattle: Seal Press.

[10] Battan, Jesse Frank (1988). The Politics of Eros: Sexual Radicalism and Social Reform in Nineteenth-Century America. Ph.D. dissertation, University of California, Los Angeles.

[11] Becker, Carol (1988). UNBROKEN TIES: Lesbian Ex-Lovers. Alyson Press.

[12] Beecher, Maureen Ursenbach and Lavina Fielding Anderson, editors (1987). SISTERS IN SPIRIT: Mormon Women in Historical and Cultural Perspective. Urbana IL: University of Illinois Press.

[13] Bennett, Kathleen (1992). "Feminist Bisexuality: A Both/ And Option for an Either/Or World" in E. R. Weise (ed) CLOSER TO HOME: BISEXUALITY AND FEMINISM. Seattle: Seal Press.

[14] Bernard, Jessie (1982). THE FUTURE OF MARRIAGE. New Haven: Yale University Press.

[15] Blank, Robert H. (1988). INDIVIDUALISM IN IDAHO: the Territorial Foundations, Pullman WA: Washington State University Press, 1988.

[16] Blasingame, Brenda Marie (1992). "The Roots of Biphobia: Racism and Internalized Heterosexism" in E.R. Weise (ed) CLOSER TO HOME: BISEXUALITY AND FEMINISM. Seattle: Seal Press.

[17] Blatt, Martin Henry (1989). FREE LOVE AND ANARCHISM: The Biography of Ezra Heywood. Urbana IL: University of Illinois Press.

[18] Bray, Gerald Lewis (1979). HOLINESS AND THE WILL OF GOD: Perspectives on the Theology of Tertullian, Atlanta: John Know Press.

[19] Brewer, Michael (1991). "Two-way Closet" in L. Hutchins and L. Kaahumanu (ed) BI ANY OTHER NAME: BISEXUAL PEOPLE SPEAK OUT. Boston: Alyson Publications.

[20] Brittain, Vera (1929). HALCYON: or, The Future of Monogamy. London: Kegan Paul, Trench, Trubner & Co., Ltd.

[21] Brown, Karen McCarthy (1991). MAMA LOLA: A Vodou Priestess in Brooklyn. Berkeley: University of California Press.

[22] Brown, Michael H. (1975). THE CASE FOR POLYGAMY. Madison Publishing.

[23] Brown, Rita Mae (1988). BINGO. New York: Bantam.

[24] Bunker, Gary L., and Davis Bitton (1983). THE MORMON GRAPHIC IMAGE, 1834-1914, Salt Lake City: University of Utah Press.

[25] Buxton, Amity Pierce (1991). THE OTHER SIDE OF THE CLOSET: THE COMING OUT CRISIS FOR STRAIGHT SPOUSES. Santa Monica, California: IBS Press.

[26] Cairncross, John (1974). AFTER POLYGAMY WAS MADE A SIN: The Social History of Christian Polygamy. London: Routledge & Kegan Paul.

[27] Choe, Margaret Mihee (1992). "Our Selves, Growing Whole" in E.R. Weise (ed) CLOSER TO HOME: BISEXUALITY AND FEMINISM. Seattle: Seal Press.

[28] Connor, Randy (1993). BLOSSOM OF BONE: Reclaiming the connection between homoeroticism and the sacred. San Francisco: Harper San Francisco.

[29] Crawford, Mary (1993). "Identity, 'Passing' and Subversion" in S. Wilkinson and C. Kitzinger (ed). HETEROSEXUALITY. London: Sage.

[30] Dada, S.A. (1986). JACOB KEHINDE COKER: Father of African Independent Churches.; Ibadan Nigeria: AOWA Printers and Publishers.

[31] Dalsimer, Marlyn Hartzell (1975). WOMEN AND FAMILY IN THE ONEIDA COMMUNITY: 1837-1881. Ph.D. Dissertation, New York University.

[32] Daly, Mary (1984). PURE LUST: Elemental Feminist Philosophy. Boston: Beacon Press.

[33] Davis, Stephen A. (1991). FUTURE SEX. Armadale, Victoria: Awareness Through Education Publishing.

[34] De Ishtar, Zohl and Zitka, Chris (ed) (1991). CONNECTING CULTURES. Sydney Lesbian Conference, Living as Lesbians – Strengthening Our Culture, July.

[35] DeMaria, Richard (1978). COMMUNAL LOVE AT ONEIDA: A Perfectionist Vision of Authority, Property, and Sexual Order. New York: Edwin Mellen Press.

[36] Dendy, David (1994). "Journey of Desire" in XY: MEN, SEX, POLITICS. Vol. 4, No.1 (Autumn), 14–16.

[37] Diamond, Milton (1992). SEX WATCHING: Looking into the world of sexual behaviour. Prion.

[38] Dixon J. (1985). "Sexuality and Relationship Changes in Married Females Following the Commencement of Bisexual Activity" in TWO LIVES TO LEAD: Bisexuality in Men and Women, Klein F., Wolf T. J. (Eds.). The Haworth Press, 115 – 133.

[39] Dowell, Susan (1987). "Jealous God? Towards a Feminist Model of Monogamy", in SEX AND GOD: Some Varieties of Women's

Religious Experience. edited Linda Hurcombe. London: Routledge, Kegan and Paul. pp. 206–228.

[40] Dowell, Susan (1990). THEY TWO SHALL BE ONE: Monogamy in History and Religion. London: Collins Flame.

[41] Ehrenberg M. (1989). WOMEN IN PREHISTORY. British Museum Publications.

[42] Elliott, Beth (1992). "Holly Near and Yet So Far" in E.R. Weise (ed) CLOSER TO HOME: BISEXUALITY AND FEMINISM. Seattle: Seal Press.

[43] Embry, Jessie L. (1987). MORMON POLYGAMOUS FAMILIES: Life in the Principle. Salt Lake City: University of Utah Press.

[44] Farley, Tucker Pamella (1985). "Lesbianism and the Social Function of Taboo" in H. Eisenstein and A. Jardine (ed) THE FUTURE OF DIFFERENCE. New Brunswick: Rutgers University Press.

[45] Farrell, Warren (1988). WHY MEN ARE THE WAY THEY ARE. New York: Berkeley Books.

[46] Feuerstein, Georg (1992). SACRED SEXUALITY: Living the Vision of the Erotic Spirit. Los Angeles: Jeremy Tarcher.

[47] Flax, Jane (1987). "Postmodernism and Gender Relations in Feminist Theory". SIGNS: JOURNAL OF WOMEN IN CULTURE AND SOCIETY 12(4): 621–643.

[48] Foster, Lawrence (1991). WOMEN, FAMILY, AND UTOPIA: Communal Experiments of the Shakers, the Oneida Community, and the Mormons. Syracuse NY: Syracuse University Press.

[49] Fourier, Charles (1967). NOUVEAU MONDE AMOUREUX. Paris: J.J. Pauvert.

[50] Gays and Lesbians Aboriginal Alliance (1994). "Peopling the Empty Mirror: The Prospects for Lesbian and Gay Aboriginal History", in R. Aldrich (ed) GAY PERSPECTIVES II. Sydney, University of Sydney.

[51] Geller, Gloria (1983). "The issue of nonmonogamy among Lesbians". RESOURCES FOR FEMINIST RESEARCH. Vol.12, No.1, 44–45.

[52] Geller, Thomas (ed) (1990). BISEXUALITY: A READER AND SOURCEBOOK. Ojai, California: TimesChange Press.

[53] George, Sue (1992). WOMEN AND BISEXUALITY. London: Scarlet Press.

[54] Gibian, Ruth (1992). "Refusing Certainty: Toward a Bisexuality of Wholeness" in E.R. Weise (ed) CLOSER TO HOME: BISEXUALITY AND FEMINISM. Seattle: Seal Press.

[55] Gillis J. (1985). FOR BETTER, FOR WORSE: British Marriages 1600 to the Present. Oxford University Press.

[56] Gimbutas, Marija (1982). THE GODDESSES AND GODS OF OLD EUROPE, 6500-3500 BC: Myths and Cult Images. New edition. Berkeley: University of California Press.

[57] Gimbutas, Marija (1989). THE LANGUAGE OF THE GODDESS: Unearthing the Hidden Symbols of Western Civilization. San Francisco: Harper and Row.

[58] Gochros, Jean Schaar (1989). WHEN HUSBANDS COME OUT OF THE CLOSET. New York: Haworth Press.

[59] Golden, Carla (1987). "Diversity and Variability in Women's Sexual Identities" in Boston Lesbian Psychologies Collective (ed) LESBIAN PSYCHOLOGIES: EXPLORATION AND CHALLENGES. Chicago: University of Illinois Press.

[60] Gollain F (1995). "Bisexuality in the Arab World" in BISEXUAL HORIZONS, Off Pink Collective (Eds.). London: Lawrence and Wishart.

[61] Goss, Robert (1993). JESUS ACTED UP: a Gay and Lesbian Manifesto. San Francisco: Harper.

[62] Grahn, Judy (1984). ANOTHER MOTHER TONGUE: Gay Words, Gay Worlds. Boston: Beacon Press.

[63] Hardy, B. Carmon (1992). SOLEMN COVENANT: The Mormon Polygamous Passage. Urbana: University of Illinois Press.

[64] Heinlein, Robert A. (1987). TO SAIL BEYOND THE SUNSET: THE LIVES AND LOVES OF MAUREEN JOHNSON. London: Michael Joseph.

[65] Helander, Gunnar (1958). MUST WE INTRODUCE MONOGAMY? A study of polygamy as a mission problem in South Africa. Pietermaritzburg: Shuter and Shooter.

[66] Hillman, Eugene (1975). POLYGAMY RECONSIDERED: African Plural marriages and the Christian Churches. Maryknoll NY: Orbis Books.

[67] Himelhoch, Bill (1990). "The Bisexual Potential" in T. Geller (ed) BISEXUALITY: A READER AND SOURCEBOOK. Ojai, California: TimesChange Press.

[68] Hite, Shere (1974). SEXUAL HONESTY, BY WOMEN FOR WOMEN. Warner Books.

[69] Hite, Shere (1994). REPORT ON THE FAMILY. Bloomsbury.

[70] Hoagland, Sarah Lucia (1988). LESBIAN ETHICS: Towards New Value. Palo Alto CA: Institute of Lesbian Studies.

[71] Hodgkinson, Liz (1988). UNHOLY MATRIMONY. Columbus.

[72] Huggins, Jackie (1994). "Alone Again ... Naturally" in D. Spender (ed) WEDDINGS AND WIVES. Melbourne: Penguin.

[73] Hurcombe, Linda, editor (1987). SEX AND GOD: Some Varieties of Women's Religious Experience, London: Routledge and Kegan Paul.

[74] Jacklin, Carol Nagy (1993). "How My Heterosexuality Affects My Feminist Politics" in S. Wilkinson and C. Kitzinger (ed) HETEROSEXUALITY. London: Sage.

[75] Janus S. S., Janus C. L. (1993). THE JANUS REPORT ON SEXUAL BEHAVIOUR. John Wiley.

[76] Johnson, Sonia (1991). THE SHIP THAT SAILED INTO THE LIVING ROOM. Estancia, New Mexico: Wildfire Books.

[77] Kern, Louis J. (1981). AN ORDERED LOVE: Sex Roles and Sexuality in Victorian Utopias: the Shakers, the Mormons, and the Oneida Community. Chapel Hill: University of North Carolina Press.

[78] Kitch, Sally (1989). CHASTE LIBERATION: Celibacy and female cultural status. Urbana: University of Illinois Press.

[79] Lewis, Jill (1982). "The Politics of Monogamy" in S. Friedman and E. Sarah (ed) ON THE PROBLEM OF MEN. London: Women's Press.

[80] Lorde, Audre (1982). ZAMI: A New Spelling of My Name, Freedom CA: Crossing Press.

[81] Mead, Margaret (1954). COMING OF AGE IN SAMOA. London: Penguin.

[82] Meekosha, Helen and Pettman, Jan (1990). "Beyond Category Politics". Paper courtesy of Jan Pettman.

[83] Miller, Leo (1974). JOHN MILTON AMONG THE POLYGAMOPHILES. New York: Loewenthal Press.

[84] Murphy, Marilyn (1990). "Thinking About Bisexuality" RESOURCES FOR FEMINIST RESEARCH 19(3/4): 87–88.

[85] Myerson, Joel, editor (1987). THE BROOK-FARM BOOK: A Collection of First-Hand Accounts of the Community. New York: Garland.

[86] Nahas, Rebecca and Turley, Myra (1979). THE NEW COUPLE: WOMEN AND GAY MEN. New York: Seaview Books.

[87] Nearing, Ryam (1992). LOVING MORE: THE POLYFIDELITY PRIMER. Hawaii: PEP Publishing.

[88] Neustatter, Angela (1994). "The 90s Way of Loving". NEW WOMAN. January, 46–51.

[89] Novak, Michael (1982). "The New Ethnicity, the Cosmopolitan Ideal, the Pluralistic Personality". AUSTRALIAN INSTITUTE OF MULTICULTURAL AFFAIRS PAPER, Melbourne.

[90] O'Dea, Thomas F. (1957). THE MORMONS. Chicago: University of Chicago Press.

[91] Orlando, Lisa (1991). "Loving Whom We Choose" in L. Hutchins and L. Kaahumanu (ed) BI ANY OTHER NAME: BISEXUAL PEOPLE SPEAK OUT. Boston: Alyson Publications.

[92] Pallotta-Chiarolli, Maria (1991). SOMEONE YOU KNOW. Adelaide: Wakefield Press.

[93] Pallotta-Chiarolli, Maria (1992). "What About Me? A Study of Italian Lesbians" in K. Herne, J. Travaglia and E. Weiss (ed) WHO DO YOU THINK YOU ARE? SECOND GENERATION IMMIGRANT WOMEN IN AUSTRALIA. Sydney: Women's Redress Press.

[94] Pallotta-Chiarolli, Maria (1993). "From Universalism to Unity in Diversity: Feminist Responses to the Intersection of Ethnicity, Gender and Sexuality", LILITH: A FEMINIST HISTORY JOURNAL 8: 41-52 (Lilith Collective, University of Melbourne).

[95] Pallotta-Chiarolli, Maria (1994). "Negotiating Ethnicity, Gender and Sexuality: The Personal Identity Formation of Lesbians of Non-English Speaking Backgrounds". Masters thesis in Women's Studies published as a monograph, Multicultural Australia Papers No. 73, (Melbourne: Ecumenical Migration Centre).

[96] Parrinder, Geoffrey (1950). THE BIBLE AND POLYGAMY: A Study of Hebrew and Christian Teaching. London: S.P.C.K.

[97] Parrinder, Geoffrey (1984). WORLD RELIGIONS: From Ancient History to the Present. New York: Facts on File.

[98] Perry, Troy D., with Thomas L.P. Swicegood (1990). DON'T BE AFRAID ANYMORE: the Story of the Reverend Troy Perry and the Metropolitan Community Churches. New York: St. Martin's Press.

[99] Pettman, Jan (1986). "Race and Ethnicity in Contemporary Australia". WORKING PAPER NO.7. Centre for Multicultural Education, University of London Institute of Education and Australian Studies Centre, Institute of Commonwealth Studies.

[100] Procter-Smith, Marjorie (1985). WOMEN IN SHAKER COMMUNITY AND WORSHIP: A Feminist Analysis of the Uses of Religious Symbolism. Lewiston NY: Mellen Press.

[101] Queen, Carol (1993). "The Safe Sex Clubs", in Anything that Moves, Summer 1993.

[102] Ralston, Caroline (1988). "Polyandry, 'pollution', 'prostitution': the problems of eurocentrism and androcentrism in Polynesian studies" in B. Caine, E.A. Grosz and M. de Lepervanche (ed) CROSSING BOUNDARIES: FEMINISM AND THE CRITIQUE OF KNOWLEDGES. Sydney: Allen and Unwin.

[103] Ratti, Rakesh, editor (1993). LOTUS OF ANOTHER COLOR: an Unfolding of the South Asian Gay and Lesbian Experience. Boston: Alyson.

[104] Reibstein J., Richards M. (1992). SEXUAL ARRANGEMENTS, MARRIAGE AND AFFAIRS. Heinemann.

[105] Rodgers, Carl (1973). BECOMING PARTNERS: Marriage and its Alternatives. Constable.

[106] Roscoe, Will, editor (1988). LIVING THE SPIRIT: A Gay American Indian Anthology. New York: St. Martin's Press.

[107] Rowland, Robyn (1993). "Radical Feminist Heterosexuality: The Personal and the Political" in S. Wilkinson and C. Kitzinger (ed) HETEROSEXUALITY. London: Sage.

[108] Rudy, Kathy (1994). "Gay Sex and Christian Ethics". Unpublished paper, delivered at the American Academy of Religion National Meeting, Chicago, Illinois, November 1994.

[109] Rust, Paula C. (1992). "Who Are We and Where Do We Go From Here? Conceptualising Bisexuality" in E.R. Weise (ed) CLOSER TO HOME: BISEXUALITY AND FEMINISM. Seattle: Seal Press.

[110] Saalfield, Catherine (1993). "Lesbian Marriage ... (K)NOT!", in Arlene Stein (ed) SISTERS, SEXPERTS, QUEERS: beyond the lesbian nation. New York: Plume.

[111] Scholem, Gershom (1946). MAJOR TRENDS IN JEWISH MYSTICISM, New York: Schoken.

[112] Schur, Edwin M. (1983). LABELING WOMEN DEVIANT: GENDER, STIGMA, AND SOCIAL CONTROL. Philadelphia: Temple University Press.

[113] Segal, Lynne (1990). SLOW MOTION: Changing Men, Changing Masculinities. London: Virago.

[114] Shuster, Rebecca (1987). "Sexuality as a Continuum: The Bisexual Identity" in Boston Lesbian Psychologies Collective (ed) LESBIAN PSYCHOLOGIES: EXPLORATIONS AND CHALLENGES. Chicago: University of Illinois Press.

[115] Shuster, Rebecca (1991). "Beyond Defense: Considering next steps for bisexual liberation" in L. Hutchins and L. Kaahumanu (ed) BI ANY OTHER NAME: BISEXUAL PEOPLE SPEAK OUT. Boston: Alyson Publications.

[116] Simenauer J., Carroll D. (1982). SINGLES: The New Americans. New York: Simon and Schuster.

[117] Smyth, Cherry (1992). LESBIANS TALK QUEER NOTIONS. London: Scarlet Press.

[118] Starhawk (1979). THE SPIRAL DANCE: A Rebirth of the Ancient Religion of the Great Goddess. San Francisco: Harper.

[119] Talbot, David (1992). "Unspeakable Pleasures" in D. Anapol (ed) LOVE WITHOUT LIMITS: THE QUEST FOR SUSTAINABLE INTIMATE RELATIONSHIPS. San Rafael, California: Intinet Resource Center.

[120] Teish, Luisah (1985). JAMBALAYA: The Natural Woman's Book. San Francisco: Harper Collins.

[121] Thompson, Denise (1993). "Against the Dividing of Women: Lesbian Feminism and Heterosexuality" in S. Wilkinson and C. Kitzinger (ed) HETEROSEXUALITY. London: Sage.

[122] Turney, Carl (1993). "Polyfidelity: Relationships of the Future" in CONSCIOUS LIVING. Feb/March: 26–27.

[123] Tertullian (1956). TREATISES ON MARRIAGE AND REMARRIAGE: To His Wife; An Exhortation to Chastity; Monogamy. translated by William P. Le Saint. Westminster MD: The Newman Press.

[124] Timothy, H.B. (1973). THE EARLY CHRISTIAN APOLOGISTS AND GREEK PHILOSOPHY: Exemplified by Irenaeus,

Tertullian, and Clement of Alexandria. Assen Netherlands: Van Gorcum.

[125] Torjesen, Karen Jo (1993). WHEN WOMEN WERE PRIESTS: Women's Leadership in the Early Church and the Scandal of their Subordination. San Francisco: Harper Collins.

[126] Udis-Kessler, Amanda (1990). "Bisexuality in an Essentialist World" in T. Geller (ed) BISEXUALITY: A READER AND SOURCEBOOK. Ojai, California: Times Change Press.A

[127] van der Leeuw, Gerardus (1967). RELIGION IN ESSENCE AND MANIFESTATION. translated by J.E. Turner. Gloucester: Peter Smith, 1967 (1938).

[128] Van Wagoner, Richard S. (1989). MORMON POLYGAMY: A History. Second Edition. Salt Lake City UT: Signature Books.

[129] Weeks, Jeffrey (1987). "Questions of Identity" in P. Caplan (ed) THE CULTURAL CONSTRUCTION OF SEXUALITY. London: Tavistock.

[130] Weeks, Jeffrey (1990). COMING OUT: Homosexual Politics in Britain from the Nineteenth Century to the Present. London: Quartet Books.

[131] Weise, Elizabeth Reba (1992). CLOSER TO HOME: BISEXUALITY AND FEMINISM. Seattle: Seal Press.

[132] Wellings K., Field J., Johnson A., Wadsworth J. (1994). SEXUAL BEHAVIOUR IN BRITAIN: The National Survey of Sexual Attitudes and Lifestyles. Penguin.

[133] Wells, Merle (1978). ANTI-MORMONISM IN IDAHO: 1872-92. Provo UT: Brigham Young University Press.

[134] White, Mel (1994). STRANGER AT THE GATE: to be Gay and Christian in America. New York: Simon and Schuster.

[135] Whitney, Catherine (1990). UNCOMMON LIVES: GAY MEN AND STRAIGHT WOMEN. New York: Plume.

[136] Williams Walter L. (1986). THE SPIRIT AND THE FLESH: Sexual Diversity in American Indian Culture. Boston: Beacon Press.

[137] Winkler, Elisbeth (1993). "Loving Two Men: twice the fun or double trouble", COSMOPOLITAN, 110-112, 194-195.

[138] Wittstock, Melinda (1990). "The Best of Both Worlds and Still Nothing" in T. Geller (ed) BISEXUALITY: A READER AND SOURCEBOOK. Ojai, California: Times Change Press.

[139] Yarbrough, O. Larry (1985). NOT LIKE THE GENTILES: Marriage Rules in the Letters of Paul. Atlanta GA: Scholars Press.

[140] Yoshizaki, Amanda (1992). "Breaking the Rules: Constructing a Bisexual Feminist Marriage" in E. R. Weise (ed) CLOSER TO HOME: BISEXUALITY AND FEMINISM. Seattle: Seal Press.

[141] Young, Iris Marion (1993). "Reflections on Families in the Age of Murphy Brown: On Gender, Justice and Sexuality" in C. Di Stefano and N. Hirschman (ed) CONCEPTS IN FEMINIST POLITICAL THEORY. Westview Press.

[142] Young, Kimball (1954). ISN'T ONE WIFE ENOUGH. New York: Henry Holt & Company.

# Contributors

**Bernadette Bosky** Since graduate training in English as Duke University, Bernadette Lynn Bosky has alternated or combined teaching and writing. Her published work is primarily non-fiction, on topics from Stephen King to Renaissance alchemy and genre theory to self-esteem; she has had two pieces of fiction published, one an erotic science fiction novella. Though this is her first professional work about polyamory, she is well known for her public speaking and amateur writings on the topic, especially within science fiction fandom and on the Internet. She lives a deceptively placid life in the suburbs of New York City with her two spouses, Arthur Hlavaty and Kevin Maroney.

**Maria Pallotta-Chiarolli** writes and researches in the issues of ethnicity, gender and sexuality. She has been published in journals such as Hecate, Journal of Intercultural Studies, Gender and Education, Migration Action, Australia and New Zealand Journal of Sociology and many others. She is the author of "Someone You Know" (Wakefield Press, Adelaide, 1991). She has taught at Adelaide University and the University of South Australia in Women's Studies, Female Sexuality and Social Diversity. She is the consultant/researcher/writer for the Multicultural HIV/AIDS Education and Support Centre in Sydney.

**Emma Donoghue** Born in Dublin, 1969, Emma Donoghue has written a play based on the Lister diaries, *I Know My Own Heart*, and two novels, *Stir-Fry* (1994) and *Hood* (1995). *Passions Between Women: British Lesbian Culture, 1668–1801* was published in 1993.

**Kevin Lano** is the author of over 40 academic publications, including two books. He is a co-editor of "Beyond Sexuality" (Phoenix Press, 1992) and a member of Off Pink Publishing and Bisexuals Action on Sexual Health.

**Claire Parry** was born in Essex in 1964. She has been active in the bisexual movement since 1986. She is a regular contributor to *Bifrost*, the national bisexual magazine.

**Alison Rowan** is a long time bisexual activist, and editor of Bifrost. She identifies as a queer, non-monogamous, anarchist, pagan and her ambition is to present the unacceptable face of sexuality. She has no cats but does have her very own brain.

**Jennifer Rycenga** is Assistant Professor of Comparative Religious Studies at San Jose State University in California. Her area of specialisation is religious experience in relation to sexuality and the arts. She is also a composer, and contributed an article on the connection between lesbianism and music in the volume Queering the Pitch (ed. Philip Brett, Elizabeth Wood, and Gary Thomas, London: Routledge 1994). She works as an activist in lesbian, feminist, anti-racist, and other life-loving causes.

# Glossary

Definitions of terms and concepts as used by the authors of the articles in the book, and also adapted from sources within the poly movement such as the `alt.polyamory` internet news group.

**Distributed commitment**: form of polyamorous living arrangement whereby one person has relationships with several others who live separately from them and each other, often because of geographical separation. More generally, a situation which is closer to a network of relatively independent individuals rather than a set of traditional couples.

**Langdon chart**: a chart of who has had sex with whom (eg, in a social group), with a set of names on the chart, and lines representing sexual connections joining names as appropriate. Refinements of the basic idea include different kinds of lines that indicate existing ongoing relationships as opposed to past ones, and lines that show (when known) attractions one person has for another.

**Line marriage**: A marriage that from time to time adds younger members, eventually establishing an equilibrium population (spouses dying off at the same rate as new ones are added). This is a different form of familial immortality than the traditional one of successive generations of children.

**Open relationships**: form of polyamory in which a primary couple agree between them that they may form secondary or transient relationships with others.

**Polyandry**: Relationships between one woman and several men. Examples of societies that practice polyandry exist in South Asia and South America.

**Polyamory**: "Loving more than one". This love may be sexual, emotional, spiritual, or any combination thereof, according to the desires and agreements of the individuals involved. A "polyamorous" individual is someone who is open to the possibility of being in more than one concurrent relationship – it is a point of debate within the poly movement as to whether this can be another form of permanent self-identity in the style of an ethnic or sexual orientation identity, or if it is more fluid and contingent. A key point is that polyamory is usually considered to involve consent by all parties involved in the relationship – this distinguishes it from secret affairs or from previous forms of non-monogamy such as the use of harems.

**Polyfidelity**: Relationship involving more than two people who have made a commitment to keep the sexual activity within the group and not have outside partners.

**Polygamy**: Converse of monogamy – connotes any social arrangement of multi-partner relationships.

**Polygyny**: relationship between one man and several women, popularly termed 'polygamy' as it is the most common form of polygamy. In the famous survey of G. P. Murdoch, 193 out of 250 societies surveyed were polygynous.

**Primary**: In a hierarchical polyamorous relationship, the person with which you are most strongly linked. This may be expressed by a marriage or other legal construct.

**Secondary**: In a hierarchical polyamorous relationship, a person who is not the most strongly linked to you, but who may nevertheless be in a close relationship with you.

**Swinging**: Partner-swapping, a subculture of mainly heterosexual couples in which women may occasionally have same-sex experiences but men very rarely do. Popularly known as 'wife-swapping' and thought to exploit women, there is some evidence that women may start to take the initiative in swinging and to benefit from this activity.

**Triad**: Polyamorous relationship consisting of three people.

**Triangle**: triad where each person is involved with each of the others, with no large differences in the degree of these involvements.

**Vee**: Relationship between three people where one person is closer to the other two than they are to each other. For instance, the 'pivot' of the vee may be the primary, within this relationship, of the other two, and they may be each other's secondary partner. Contrast with triangle.

# Resources and Groups

## Activism

The poly movement is a very recent phenomenon, and is only organised on a significant scale in the USA, but is likely to expand in the future as more information and experience regarding polyamory becomes available.

## USA

In the USA groups discussing and organising social support for responsible non-monogamous lifestyles date back to the counter-culture of the 1960's. The 'Church of all Worlds' is an example of such an organisation – founded in 1962 and inspired by Heinlein's *Stranger in a Strange Land*, it is a goddess/nature spirituality group with non-monogamy being fully accepted. They publish *Green Egg*. A variety of similar new-age groups with philosophies supporting non-monogamy exist across the US (eg, 'Family Synergy', 'Family Tree', 'More University', etc – see (Anapol, 1992) for more details). Some non-monogamous communes from the 1960s survived into the 90's, such as Kerista, which was based on multiple group marriages and rotational sleeping schedules, and who originated the term 'polyfidelity'. The science fiction community, via its national and international fan conferences, also served as an informal meeting ground for many people interested in putting into practice some of the alternative poly lifestyles described by authors such as Heinlein, Marion Zimmer Bradley (The Forbidden Tower) and Robert Rimmer (The Harrad Experiment, Proposition 31, etc).

Local support groups for people involved in polyamorous relationships exist in a large number of cities and towns in the US, such as Philadelphia, Milwaukee, Washington, etc. These groups tend to be based around discussion sessions and social events such as potlucks and dinners. At a regional and national level the most established of the poly networks is 'IntiNet Resources Center' in California which aims to provide resources and information for people exploring responsible non-monogamy. It published the book *Love Without Limits* and produces the *Floodtide* newsletter. PEP (polyfidelitous educational productions) in Hawaii performs a similar role for those involved in polyfidelitous relationships.

National poly conferences began with PEP's 1987 conference in Oregon, and are now an annual event, attracting hundreds of participants. The 1994 PEPCON in Oakland attracted 130 participants and had an increased involvement from bisexuals and lesbians. It had sessions on the theory of non-monogamy, issues involved in starting support groups, therapy, gender conflict, and on tantra and spirituality. Poly issues are also regularly discussed at conferences on alternative lifestyles, paganism and sexuality. The poly community typically intersects quite strongly with other alternative communities such as the pagan or bisexual communities. There are links also to the SM culture. In some places (eg, Milwaukee), its sometimes hard to separate the sexual and relationship ties between people from the political communities – people will turn up to group meetings where they've slept with everyone else in the room .... This can cause problems when relationships go bad: you not only lose your lovers, you are excluded from the community as well!

Electronic networking is also most advanced in the US, with a number of mailing lists and bulletin boards dealing with aspects of poly life. Leading figures from the poly movement, such as Deborah Anapol and Paul Glassco from IntiNet, have appeared on talk shows such as Donahue and Joan Rivers.

The organisation of safe-sex clubs in San Francisco and the East Coast can also be seen as part of the poly movement, although the initiative for these clubs came from the bisexual and queer communities. According to Carol Queen (Queen, 1993):

> *"It was November 1987. People were growing tired of the way the AIDS crisis had made sex fearsome for so many. Beneath the quiet, grieving facade of the 80's, a new sexual revolution had been fermenting.*
> 
> *Word went out all over the bay area sex community. Nothing like this multi-gendered, omni-persuasional, and safe had ever been tried. It wasn't a jack-off party – women would be there. Not a swing party – gay men would be included, fucking would not. Not a freewheeling '70s orgy*

> *– those hadn't been run by strict safe sex rules. It wasn't like anything, except maybe the future. It was a new forum for radical sex in uncertain times."*

A variety of clubs have existed, from the Club Eros (mixed and open to the public) to the monthly Jack-and-Jill-Offs sponsored by Mother Goose Productions. The latter, faced with an extremely high male-to-female ratio at its parties, instituted the "New School for Social Masturbation" which trains people in how to negotiate safer sex before they can go on to participate in the parties.

## Australia

In Australia there is a support network for polyamorous people, called 'Beyond Monogamy', based in Perth. It provides information and social groups, and has over 70 member individuals or partnerships. The article (Turney, 1993) is by one of the founders of this organisation.

Other poly work in Australia includes the making of a documentary video called "In Bed with Your Neighbours". On safe sex, education and non-monogamy issues, this was produced in 1994 by Quality Productions, New South Wales, and was put on national release in Australia.

## UK

Discussions on poly issues have taken place within the lesbian and gay and bisexual movements, and workshops on non-monogamy are a regular feature of the annual bisexual conference. No local poly support groups are known to the editors at the present time, although there is some UK participation in alt.polyamory.

There has been a campaign at Royal Holloway college in London for poly issues to be addressed by the student welfare office, with some success.

# Groups

## USA

**IntiNet Resource Center**: Box 4322 San Rafael, CA 94913.
**Hawaii**: Polyfidelitous Educational Productions P.O. Box 6306 Captain Cook, HI 96704-6306.

**San Jose**: SOUTH BAY INTINET, P.O. BOX 70203, Sunnyvale, CA 94086. Email: bwabsc@tevm2.nsc.com: monthly discussion and support group, produce newsletter.

There are also groups in San Francisco, Oregon, Nashville and Baltimore.

Swing clubs and organisations are:

**North America Swing Club Association**, P.O. Box 7128, Buena Park, CA 90622.

**SSC Magazine**, P.O. Box 459, San Dimas, CA 91773.

## Germany

**ZEGG**: "Zentrum fuer Experimentelle Gesellschaftsgestaltung", or "The Center for Experimental Cultural Design". Its main headquarters is about 60 miles southwest of Berlin.

# Electronic

**alt.polyamory**: Internet news group, discusses the issues and is very supportive.

**triples-request@hal.com**: Triples mailing list. Send mail to this address if you'd like to be included on the list.

# Books

These are books recommended on alt.polyamory, with some additions by the editors. The grading scheme follows that of the group (list compiled by Holly Wilper).

## Non-fiction

The degree of poly relevance is indicated by the number of *'s, the degree of poly friendliness by the number of !'s.

```
*****  !!!!!  Deborah Anapol, "Love Without Limits"
*****  !!!!!  M. L. Carden, "Oneida : Utopian Community
               to Modern Corporation"
*****  !     Audrey Chapman, "Mansharing : Dilemma or Choice"
*****  !!!!  G. Clanton & C. Downing, "Face to Face to Face"
*****  !!    L. & J. Constantine, "Group Marriage"
***    !!!!! Samuel R. Delany, "Heavenly Breakfast"
***    !!!!! Samuel R. Delany, "The Motion of Light in Water"
**     !!    Milton Diamond, "Sex Watching : Looking into the
               world of sexual behaviour"
**     !!    Margaret Ehrenberg, "Women in Prehistory"
**     !!!!  Helen Fisher, "Anatomy of Love"
**     !!!   Liz Hodgkinson, "Unholy Matrimony"
*      !     Arno Karlen, "Threesomes : Studies in Sex,
               Power, and Intimacy"
```

*Resources and Groups*

```
•••••  !!!!!  Aidan A. Kelly (ed), "The New Polygamy: The Polyamorous
               Lifestyle as a New Spiritual Path."
•••    !!!    R. Libby & R. Whitehurst, "Marriage and Alternatives:
               Exploring Intimate Relationships"
•••    !!!    R. Mazur, "The New Intimacy: Open Marriages
               and Alternative Lifestyles"
••     !      Peter McWilliams, "Ain't Nobody's Business If You Do: The
               Absurdity of Consensual Crimes in a Free Society"
•••••  !!!!!  Ryam Nearing, "Loving More: The Polyfidelity Primer"
               (see PEP listing under organisations)
••••   !!!!!  Nena and George O'Neill, "Open Marriage"
•••    n/a    "The Pillow Book" (erotic art from India, China, and Japan)
•••    !!!    James Ramey, "Intimate Friendships"
•••    !!     Janet Reibstein, Martin Richards, "Sexual Arrangements,
               Marriage and Affairs"
•••    !!!    Carl Rogers, "Becoming Partners: Marriage and Its
               Alternatives"
••     !!!!   Bertrand Russell, "Marriage and Morals"
•••••  !!!    Gay Talese, "Thy Neighbor's Wife"
•••    !      Robert Thamm, "Beyond Marriage and the Nuclear Family"
```

# Fiction

Grading system is as above.

```
•      !      Isabel Allende, "Eva Luna"
•••    !!     Thea Alexander, "2150 AD"
••     !!     Wilhelmina Baird, "Crashcourse"
•••    !!!    John Dudley Ball, "Chief Tallon and the S.O.R."
•••    !!!    M. A. R. Barker, "Flamesong"
•••    !!!    M. A. R. Barker, "Man of Gold"
•••••  !!!!   Gael Baudino, "Gossamer Axe"
•••••  !!!!!  Amy Bloom, "Love is Not a Pie", short story
•••    !!!!   Marion Zimmer Bradley, "The Forbidden Tower"
••     !!     Rita Mae Brown, "Six of One"
••     !!!    Ernest Callenbach, "Ecotopia"
••     !!!    Ernest Callenbach, "Ecotopia Emerging"
••     !!!!!  Samuel R. Delany, "Babel – 17"
•      !!!    Samuel R. Delany, "Dhalgren"
•      !!!!!  Samuel R. Delany, "Stars in My Pocket Like Grains of Sand"
••     !!!    Samuel R. Delany, "Triton"
••     !!!    Wayne Dyer, "Gifts From Eykis"
•••    !!!    Robert Graves, "Goodbye to All That"
•••    !!!    Robert Graves, "Watch the North Wind Rise"
••     !!!!!  Robert Heinlein, "Beyond This Horizon"
••     !!!!!  Robert Heinlein, "The Cat Who Walked Through Walls"
••     !!!!!  Robert Heinlein, "Friday"
•••    !!!!!  Robert Heinlein, "Glory Road"
••••   !!!!!  Robert Heinlein, "I Will Fear No Evil"
•••    !!!!!  Robert Heinlein, "Methuselah's Children"
••     !!!!!  Robert Heinlein, "The Moon is a Harsh Mistress"
•••    !!!!!  Robert Heinlein, "To Sail Beyond the Sunset"
••••   !!!!!  Robert Heinlein, "Stranger in a Strange Land"
•••    !!     Mercedes Lackey & Ellen Guon, "Knight of Ghosts and Shadows"
••     !!!!   Doris Lessing, "The Marriages Between Zones Three, Four,
               and Five"
•••    !!     Elizabeth Lynn, "The Dancers of Arun"
•••    !!     Elizabeth Lynn, "A Different Light"
•••    !!     Elizabeth Lynn, "The Sardonyx Net"
••••   !!!!   Donald Kingsbury, "Courtship Rite" ("Geta" in the UK)
••••   !!!!   Milan Kundera, "The Unbearable Lightness of Being"
••••   !!!    Michael P. Kube – McDowell, "The Quiet Pools"
••••   !!!!   Larry McMurty, "Leaving Cheyenne"
••     !!!    Vonda McIntyre, "Starfarers"
••     !!!    Vonda McIntyre, "Transition"
••     !!!    Vonda McIntyre, "Metaphase"
•      !      Vladimir Nabokov, "Ada"
••••   !      Maxine Paetro, "Manshare"
•      !!!    David Palmer, "Emergence"
••••   !!!!   Marge Piercy, "The High Cost of Living"
•••    !!     Marge Piercy, "Woman on the Edge of Time"
••••   !!!    Marge Piercy, "Summer People"
•••••  !!!!!  Robert Rimmer, "Come Live My Life"
```

|  |  |  |
|---|---|---|
| •••• | !!!!! | Robert Rimmer, "The Harrad Experiment" |
| ••• | !!!!! | Robert Rimmer, "The Immoral Reverend" |
| ••• | !!!!! | Robert Rimmer, "The Love Exchange" |
| ••• | !!!!! | Robert Rimmer, "Premar Experiments" |
| ••• | !!!!! | Robert Rimmer, "Proposition 31" |
| ••• | !!!!! | Robert Rimmer, "The Rebellion of Yale Marrat" |
| •••• | !!!!! | Robert Rimmer, "Thursday My Love" |
| •• | !! | Elizabeth Scarbourough, "The Harem of Aman Akbar" |
| ••• | !!!!! | Starhawk, "The Fifth Sacred Thing" |
| •• | !!! | John Varley, Gaia trilogy; "Demon", "Titan", "Wizard" |
| •• | !!! | John Varley, "The Persistance of Vision" |
| •• | !!! | Alice Walker, "The Temple of My Familiar" |
| ••• | !!! | James Wharram, "Two Girls, Two Catamarans" |

## Movies

Reviews taken from alt.polyamory.

**Another Woman's Lipstick** (Denise Crosby). Three episodes based on "Red Shoe Diaries", first episode concerns a woman who has two different lovers, who satisfy different needs. More dishonest monogamy than polyamory.

**Belle Epoque** Spanish film set during the Spanish Civil War. An artist takes in a deserter, who repays him by sleeping with all four of his daughters. It's pretty light hearted and a warm farcical romp.

**Bob and Carol and Ted and Alice** (Robert Culp, Angie Dickenson). More a wife-swapping talk than any model for a healthy poly relationship. Still, widely known and raises poly questions.

**Cabaret** (Liza Minelli, Michael York, Joel Grey). A not-very-honest triad is part of the plot

**A Change of Seasons** (Shirley Maclaine, Bo Derek). Maclaine's professor husband has an affair with Derek; she then has an affair of her own, and then the four decide to go on a holiday together to see whether they can work something out ...

**Enemies: A Love Story** (Angelica Houston, Ron Silver). A tale of a man and the three women in his life.

**The Harrad Experiment** (James Whitmore, Tippi Hedron, Don Johnson). Adaptation of the Robert Rimmer book. Unfortunately it spends so much time on the topic of public nudity that it has little left over to deal with poly issues.

**Heartbeat**  (Nick Nolte). This is the story of "beat" reporter Jack Kerouac's affair with a married couple.

**Henry and June**  (Uma Thurman, Fred Ward). Writer Henry Miller has an affair with his friend Anais Nin ... and then his wife June shows up. Anais finds herself becoming attracted to June ...

**The Hunger**  (Catherine Deneuve, David Bowie, Susan Sarandon). More bi than poly, and only a few moments of that. At the end Sarandon's character seems to have new lovers of both genders.

**A Lesson in Love**  (1954) (Ingmar Bergman). A romantic comedy about a doctor trying to win back his wife after she leaves him over an affair of his.

**Lianna**  (John Sayles). A professor's wife finds out he's having an affair, and at the same time falls in love with a female professor. More a lesbian tale than a poly one, but especially good at showing the effects on family and friends of "coming out" different.

**Loving Molly**  (Beau Bridges, Sally Fields). The story of three men and the one woman that they share from the time they are children and throughout their lives.

**Lucky Lady**  (Liza Minelli, Gene Hackman, Burt Reynolds). It does look like the three main characters are getting set to stay together at the end of the movie.

**Mahabharata**  Contains the marriage of five brothers, the Pandava, to a single wife, Draupadi, based (I believe) on aspects of mythology from India.

**No Way Out**  (Kevin Costner, Sean Young, Gene Hackman). Costner gets involved with Young, who is already involved with his boss (Hackman). Bad things happen. She actively says that she is poly (before she is killed).

**Paint Your Wagon**  (Lee Marvin, Jane Fonda, Clint Eastwood). Due to the scarcity of women, Marvin and Eastwood share one.

**Red Shoe Diaries** Man finds out about girlfriends poly lifestyle after she kills herself. Then he meets her other lover.

**Rita and Sue ... and Bob too** A married man's affair with two younger women causes his wife to leave him. Can the three lovers transmute their sexual interest into something more lasting?

**Same Time Next Year** (Alan Alda). Alda has a once a year meeting with his lover (as opposed to his wife), most of the time is spent examining the changes in the two people in the intervening times.

**The Seduction of Joe Tynan** (Alan Alda). Alda plays a politician who falls in love with another woman at a convention.

**She's Gotta Have It** One of Spike Lee's earliest films, deals with a polyamorous young woman and the three men who want her to choose. There are also a lot of Afro-American male/female issues addressed in this movie.

**Small Circle of Friends** Genuine poly values are central to the plot of this film about a MFM triad. Low-budget production, but asks good questions.

**Summer Lovers** (Darryl Hannah). A young American couple on a summer vacation in the Mediterranean get involved with a French archaeologist.

**3 of Hearts** (this has a different ending in the European release) (Kelly Lynch, Sherilyn Fenn, William Baldwin). Lesbian Lynch loses partner Fenn, who is bi, she pays Baldwin to seduce Fenn and dump her, hoping that she will come back. In the European release the movie ends with Baldwin getting the girl, in the American release he doesn't.

**Threesome** (Laura Flynn Boyle, Steven Baldwin, Josh Charles). The story of 2 men and 1 woman who find themselves assigned to the same dorm room, and the relationship that develops. Their multi-partner relationship is portrayed in a very poly-friendly way.

**The Unbearable Lightness of Being** (Daniel Day-Lewis, Lena Olin). The womanising Tomas falls in love with the monogamous Tereza, but cannot give up his lover Sabina. ... Meanwhile, Russian tanks roll over Prague ...

# SEXUAL POLITICS TITLES FROM FIVE LEAVES PUBLICATIONS

☐ **SINEWS OF THE HEART: A BOOK OF MEN'S WRITING** Edited by Paul Devlin et al.
Paperback, 164 pages, £6.99.
Exploring the pain, passion and pleasure of being male today.
0 907123 41 4.

☐ **DESTROYING THE BABY IN THEMSELVES: WHY DID THE TWO BOYS KILL JAMES BULGER?**
by David Jackson.
Paperback, 48 pages, £3.50
0 907123 31 7

☐ **THIS IS NO BOOK: A GAY READER** by Gregory Woods.
Paperback, 112 pages, £6.95.
Essays and reviews on gay culture.
0 907123 26 0

All titles are available through bookshops or can be purchased post-free from Five Leaves Publications, PO Box 81, Nottingham, NG5 4ER.